JUMBLE®

GRAB BAG

Reach Inside for a Puzzle Surprise!

by Henri Arnold, Bob Lee, and Mike Argirion

TRIUMPH
BOOKS
CHICAGO

This book is available at special discounts
for your group or organization.

For further information, contact:
Triumph Books
601 South LaSalle Street
Suite 500
Chicago, Illinois 60605
(312) 939-3330
(312) 663-3557 FAX

ISBN 1-57243-273-X

Printed in the USA

CONTENTS

CLASSIC

DAILY

CHALLENGER

ANSWERS

JUMBLE®

Unscramble these four Jumbles,
one letter to each square, to
form four ordinary words.

LARNS

BOGUM

CROFIL

SCEBIT

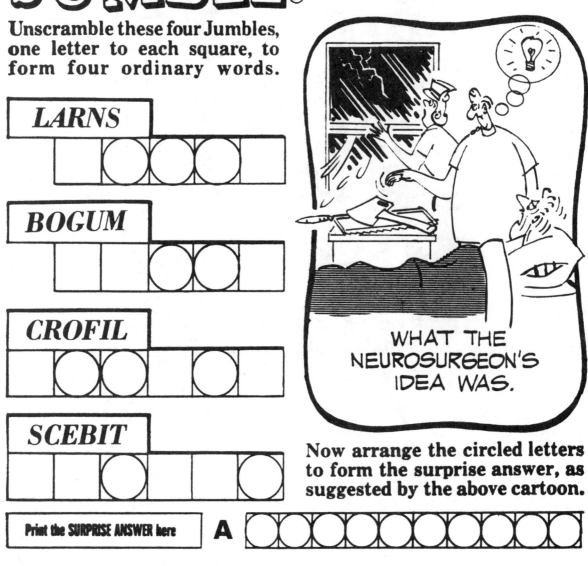

WHAT THE
NEUROSURGEON'S
IDEA WAS.

Now arrange the circled letters
to form the surprise answer, as
suggested by the above cartoon.

Print the SURPRISE ANSWER here

A

JUMBLE®

Unscramble these four Jumbles, one letter to each square, to form four ordinary words.

WONIG

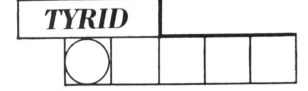

TYRID

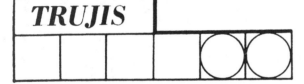

TRUJIS

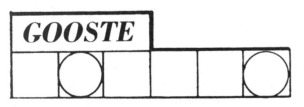

GOOSTE

Print the SURPRISE ANSWER here

Poker . . . sick friend . . . traffic

HOW THE PRETZEL MAKER GOT HIS ALIBI.

Now arrange the circled letters to form the surprise answer, as suggested by the above cartoon.

JUMBLE®

Unscramble these four Jumbles,
one letter to each square, to
form four ordinary words.

MYKUR

INHEW

YECKAL

DELPOW

. . . all a mistake
. . . didn't mean . . .

WHAT THE SNAKE IN
THE GRASS DID WHEN
HE WAS CAUGHT IN
THE ACT.

Now arrange the circled letters
to form the surprise answer, as
suggested by the above cartoon.

Print the SURPRISE
ANSWER here ☐☐☐☐☐☐☐ **HIS** ☐☐☐ **OUT**

JUMBLE®

Unscramble these four Jumbles,
one letter to each square, to
form four ordinary words.

DUTEE

RUYLS

CLAMBE

GROAFE

Ugh!

HOW THE PORTRAIT
PAINTER EXPRESSED
HIMSELF.

Now arrange the circled letters
to form the surprise answer, as
suggested by the above cartoon.

Print the SURPRISE ANSWER here **HE** ⬡⬡⬡⬡ ⬡⬡⬡⬡⬡

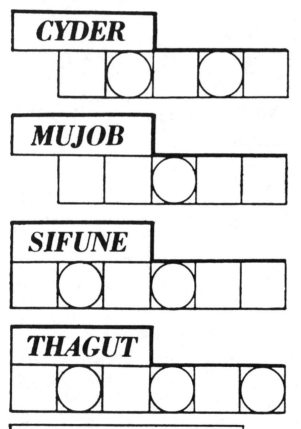

JUMBLE®

Unscramble these four Jumbles,
one letter to each square, to
form four ordinary words.

CYDER

MUJOB

SIFUNE

THAGUT

THIS COULD BE
THE DIFFERENCE
BETWEEN MALE
AND FEMALE.

Now arrange the circled letters
to form the surprise answer, as
suggested by the above cartoon.

Print the SURPRISE ANSWER here **AN**

JUMBLE®

Unscramble these four Jumbles, one letter to each square, to form four ordinary words.

HEMIC

RAHOY

WEKERS

THAGAS

Print the SURPRISE ANSWER here

SOME GI'S CONSIDER THIS THE SLOPPIEST PART OF THE ARMY.

Now arrange the circled letters to form the surprise answer, as suggested by the above cartoon.

JUMBLE®

Unscramble these four Jumbles, one letter to each square, to form four ordinary words.

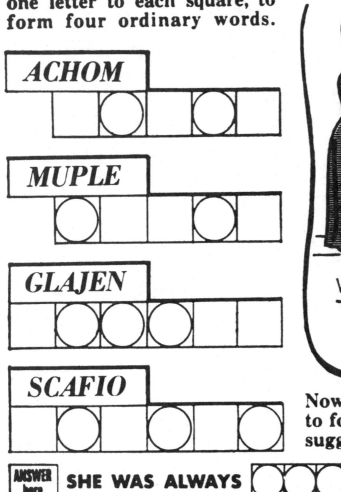

ACHOM

MUPLE

GLAJEN

SCAFIO

Again?

She'll be with you in a moment

WHY THEY CALLED THE DIZZY BLONDE "BUBBLE HEAD."

Now arrange the circled letters to form the surprise answer, as suggested by the above cartoon.

ANSWER here **SHE WAS ALWAYS**

JUMBLE®

Unscramble these four Jumbles,
one letter to each square, to
form four ordinary words.

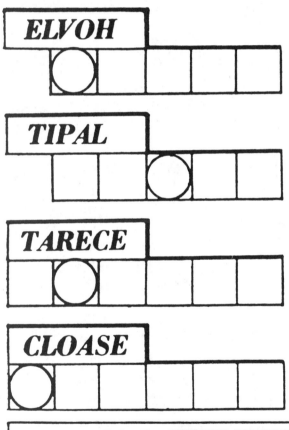

ELVOH

TIPAL

TARECE

CLOASE

Fellows . . .

THIS CAN BE
IRRITATING AS WELL
AS FOOLISH.

Now arrange the circled letters
to form the surprise answer, as
suggested by the above cartoon.

Print the SURPRISE ANSWER here

JUMBLE®

Unscramble these four Jumbles, one letter to each square, to form four ordinary words.

GURAU

HICED

TURBLE

CLAUNY

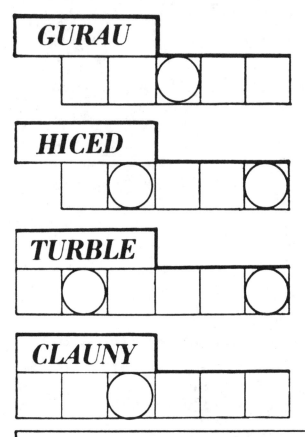

Make any money today?

THIS MIGHT MEAN NOTHING'S BEEN TAKEN IN.

Now arrange the circled letters to form the surprise answer, as suggested by the above cartoon.

Print the SURPRISE ANSWER here

JUMBLE®

Unscramble these four Jumbles, one letter to each square, to form four ordinary words.

LIWLT

YOBOT

THINGK

STEJAM

Get lost!

WHAT THE FRUSTRATED ARTIST DREW.

Now arrange the circled letters to form the surprise answer, as suggested by the above cartoon.

Print the SURPRISE ANSWER here

A

JUMBLE®

Unscramble these four Jumbles,
one letter to each square, to
form four ordinary words.

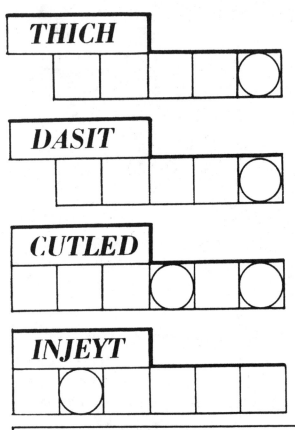

THICH

DASIT

CUTLED

INJEYT

BARBER SHOP

THIS GETS LONGER EVERY TIME YOU CUT IT.

Now arrange the circled letters
to form the surprise answer, as
suggested by the above cartoon.

Print the SURPRISE ANSWER here

A

JUMBLE®

Unscramble these four Jumbles,
one letter to each square, to
form four ordinary words.

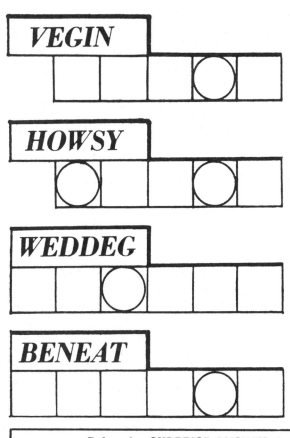

VEGIN

HOWSY

WEDDEG

BENEAT

Such a
sweeping
statement!

THIS OFTEN
COVERS A LOT!

Now arrange the circled letters
to form the surprise answer, as
suggested by the above cartoon.

Print the SURPRISE ANSWER here

JUMBLE®

Unscramble these four Jumbles,
one letter to each square, to
form four ordinary words.

HUTEC

ANUFA

BITSUM

GURDIT

WHERE A PEDESTRIAN
MIGHT FEEL ON EDGE.

Now arrange the circled letters
to form the surprise answer, as
suggested by the above cartoon.

Print the SURPRISE ANSWER here

◯◯ THE ◯◯◯◯

JUMBLE®

Unscramble these four Jumbles, one letter to each square, to form four ordinary words.

RELEC

TARIE

WOBELL

DOVERN

THIS GUY MIGHT TELL YOU A STORY WITH A SLANT TO IT.

DOC'S CURE ALL 98¢

Now arrange the circled letters to form the surprise answer, as suggested by the above cartoon.

Print the ANSWER here ONE WHO'S ◯◯◯ ON THE ◯◯◯◯◯

JUMBLE®

Unscramble these four Jumbles,
one letter to each square, to
form four ordinary words.

ETHIL

TILOP

SNAZAT

HARGIS

WHAT YOU MIGHT FIND
IN THAT OL'
SWIMMIN' HOLE.

Now arrange the circled letters
to form the surprise answer, as
suggested by the above cartoon.

Print the SURPRISE ANSWER here " ☐☐☐☐☐ – ☐☐☐☐☐ "

JUMBLE®

#16

Unscramble these four Jumbles, one letter to each square, to form four ordinary words.

MYNAL

YEJON

DISTEW

ORISEE

WHEN MOTHER SAW THE BATHROOM SHE SAID THIS.

Now arrange the circled letters to form the surprise answer, as suggested by the above cartoon.

Print the SURPRISE ANSWER here "⬡⬡⬡⬡⬡ ⬡⬡⬡⬡!"

17

JUMBLE®

Unscramble these four Jumbles,
one letter to each square, to
form four ordinary words.

LAUVE

GUDOH

CREELY

GURTIA

WHAT A CRAVAT TYCOON
MIGHT EXPECT PLENTY
OF FROM THE NEW
WIDE STYLES.

Now arrange the circled letters
to form the surprise answer, as
suggested by the above cartoon.

Print the SURPRISE ANSWER here

JUMBLE®

Unscramble these four Jumbles,
one letter to each square, to
form four ordinary words.

URRJO

CUIMS

WISDON

SUTTOM

Look . . .
guess what . . .

Oh,
shut
up!

GOSSIP CAN BE
A PAIN WHEN
IT'S THIS.

Now arrange the circled letters
to form the surprise answer, as
suggested by the above cartoon.

Print the SURPRISE ANSWER here

◯◯◯◯◯◯ – ◯◯◯◯◯

JUMBLE®

Unscramble these four Jumbles, one letter to each square, to form four ordinary words.

YARIF

DUHMI

NOPETT

CONTOY

WHAT A GUY WHO GOT COLD FEET BEFORE THE WEDDING DID.

Now arrange the circled letters to form the surprise answer, as suggested by the above cartoon.

Print the SURPRISE ANSWER here

IT

JUMBLE®

Unscramble these four Jumbles, one letter to each square, to form four ordinary words.

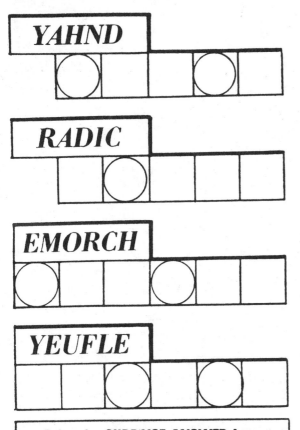

YAHND

RADIC

EMORCH

YEUFLE

Print the **SURPRISE ANSWER** here

Uh . . . mumble . . . mumble . . .

Speak freely

LANGUAGE SPOKEN BY THE PSYCHIATRIST'S PATIENT.

Now arrange the circled letters to form the surprise answer, as suggested by the above cartoon.

"⬡⬡⬡⬡⬡⬡⬡⬡"

JUMBLE®

Unscramble these four Jumbles,
one letter to each square, to
form four ordinary words.

CAPNI

GAMLE

LURSEY

ANSTUE

HOW THE CLOWN IN
THE GEOLOGY CLASS
DEFINED "BEDROCK."

Now arrange the circled letters
to form the surprise answer, as
suggested by the above cartoon.

Print the SURPRISE
ANSWER here " ◯◯◯◯◯ TO ◯◯◯◯◯ BY "

JUMBLE®

Unscramble these four Jumbles,
one letter to each square, to
form four ordinary words.

VELGA
G A V E L

AXORB
B O R A X

ZEMENY
E N Z Y M E

NOOTIL
L O T I O N

THE DELICATESSEN
MAN'S WIFE SUMMED
UP HIS ALIBI
IN ONE WORD.

Now arrange the circled letters
to form the surprise answer, as
suggested by the above cartoon.

"B A L O N E Y !"

Print the SURPRISE ANSWER here

A L B Y E O N

JUMBLE®

Unscramble these four Jumbles,
one letter to each square, to
form four ordinary words.

TULDA

TENIL

RAWSUL

QUALEP

HOW HE
PRODUCED OIL.

Now arrange the circled letters
to form the surprise answer, as
suggested by the above cartoon.

Print the SURPRISE ANSWER here

JUMBLE®

Unscramble these four Jumbles,
one letter to each square, to
form four ordinary words.

PEALL

SELBS

REPOOC

PANPHE

HOW THE BANANA
TYCOON LOST
A LAWSUIT.

Now arrange the circled letters
to form the surprise answer, as
suggested by the above cartoon.

Print the SURPRISE ANSWER here

◯◯ A ◯◯◯◯◯

JUMBLE®

Unscramble these four Jumbles,
one letter to each square, to
form four ordinary words.

EGBOY

HOYNE

SOUREA

RUBETT

WHAT THEY WERE IN
THE NURSERY.

Now arrange the circled letters
to form the surprise answer, as
suggested by the above cartoon.

Print the SURPRISE
ANSWER here

⬭⬭⬭⬭⬭⬭ **AS** ⬭⬭⬭⬭⬭

JUMBLE®

Unscramble these four Jumbles,
one letter to each square, to
form four ordinary words.

YARDT

HESEP

MOANAZ

TRUIPY

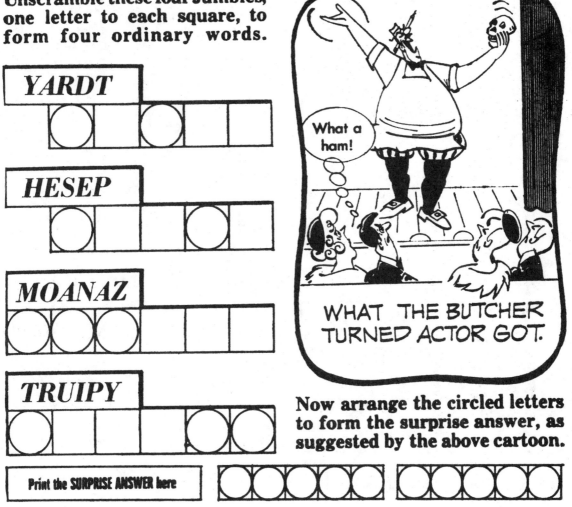

What a ham!

WHAT THE BUTCHER
TURNED ACTOR GOT.

Now arrange the circled letters
to form the surprise answer, as
suggested by the above cartoon.

Print the SURPRISE ANSWER here

JUMBLE®

Unscramble these four Jumbles,
one letter to each square, to
form four ordinary words.

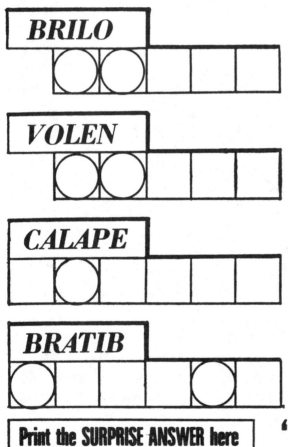

BRILO

VOLEN

CALAPE

BRATIB

WHAT THE BABY WHO
FIRST SAW THE LIGHT OF
DAY ON A PLANE WAS.

Now arrange the circled letters
to form the surprise answer, as
suggested by the above cartoon.

Print the SURPRISE ANSWER here

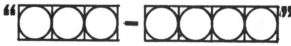

"◯◯◯ - ◯◯◯◯"

JUMBLE®

Unscramble these four Jumbles, one letter to each square, to form four ordinary words.

ROMAR

LYBUL

MEAFED

ABHORR

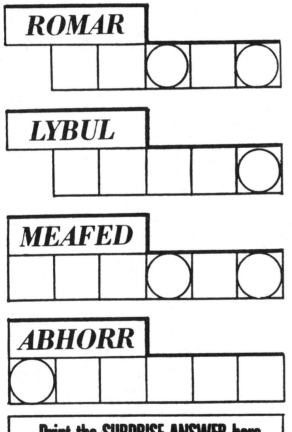

Print the SURPRISE ANSWER here

THE ALCOHOLIC ACTOR'S FAVORITE SANDWICH.

Now arrange the circled letters to form the surprise answer, as suggested by the above cartoon.

 **ON**

JUMBLE®

Unscramble these four Jumbles,
one letter to each square, to
form four ordinary words.

OSLOE

CLAME

LAFTER

TEECIX

WHAT A FAT MAN IN A
TELEPHONE BOOTH
MIGHT SUGGEST.

Now arrange the circled letters
to form the surprise answer, as
suggested by the above cartoon.

Print the SURPRISE ANSWER here   A

JUMBLE®

Unscramble these four Jumbles, one letter to each square, to form four ordinary words.

VILEA

NUKKS

REMUDE

SEPPOO

My, my!

WHAT A LITTLE SOFT SOAP CAN MAKE.

Now arrange the circled letters to form the surprise answer, as suggested by the above cartoon.

Print the SURPRISE ANSWER here

A ◯◯◯◯ ◯◯◯◯◯

JUMBLE®

Unscramble these four Jumbles, one letter to each square, to form four ordinary words.

COEMA

OMPET

BANACA

EPITOC

WHAT SOME POLITICIANS SEEM TO WANT TO TAX MOST.

Now arrange the circled letters to form the surprise answer, as suggested by the above cartoon.

Print the SURPRISE ANSWER here: **OUR**

JUMBLE®

Unscramble these four Jumbles, one letter to each square, to form four ordinary words.

RICOU

KOSTE

THODEB

NATIED

THE DEBTOR'S MOTTO.

Now arrange the circled letters to form the surprise answer, as suggested by the above cartoon.

Print the SURPRISE ANSWER here

" ☐☐☐ UNTO ☐☐☐☐☐☐☐ "

JUMBLE®

Unscramble these four Jumbles, one letter to each square, to form four ordinary words.

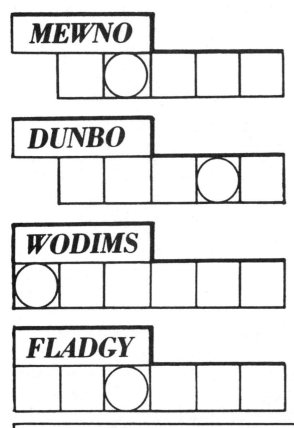

MEWNO

DUNBO

WODIMS

FLADGY

OK

Sick . . . can't get up to go to school . . .

LYING LIKE THIS CAN BE EASY!

Now arrange the circled letters to form the surprise answer, as suggested by the above cartoon.

Print the SURPRISE ANSWER here

JUMBLE®

Unscramble these four Jumbles,
one letter to each square, to
form four ordinary words.

ACCOO

NONAY

PREFIL

CITILE

Great
story—
human
interest

IN THE LONG RUN,
THIS WILL BENEFIT
A WRITER!

Now arrange the circled letters
to form the surprise answer, as
suggested by the above cartoon.

Print the SURPRISE ANSWER here

JUMBLE®

Unscramble these four Jumbles, one letter to each square, to form four ordinary words.

NAJOB

FREVE

YELLIK

TIVNAY

WHAT THE STORY OF THE BELLY DANCER WAS.

Now arrange the circled letters to form the surprise answer, as suggested by the above cartoon.

Print the SURPRISE ANSWER here

A ◯◯◯◯◯◯ ◯◯◯◯◯

JUMBLE®

Unscramble these four Jumbles,
one letter to each square, to
form four ordinary words.

LOGAT

Ⓖ Ⓛ O A T

YAHIR

H A Ⓘ R Y

NIPURT

Ⓣ U R N I P

HESTEE

S E E T Ⓗ E

That'll wow him!

SHEER BLOUSES

TO GET A HEAVY
DATE WEAR THIS.

Now arrange the circled letters
to form the surprise answer, as
suggested by the above cartoon.

Print the SURPRISE ANSWER here

SOMETHING Ⓛ Ⓘ Ⓖ Ⓗ Ⓣ

JUMBLE®

Unscramble these four Jumbles, one letter to each square, to form four ordinary words.

CEEPA

VORSA

SEPORC

ROAMON

THIS CAN MAKE A HASH OF MARRIAGE.

Now arrange the circled letters to form the surprise answer, as suggested by the above cartoon.

Print the SURPRISE ANSWER here

JUMBLE®

Unscramble these four Jumbles, one letter to each square, to form four ordinary words.

KREAM

NARFC

INLOOT

RAMPHE

WHAT A CRIMEAN BECAME AFTER RECEIVING HIS CITIZENSHIP PAPERS.

Now arrange the circled letters to form the surprise answer, as suggested by the above cartoon.

Print answer here: " ◯◯◯◯◯◯◯◯◯ "

JUMBLE®

Unscramble these four Jumbles,
one letter to each square, to form
four ordinary words.

REBBI

HOPOW

SLIZZE

PERMAC

WHAT THE POLICE—
WOMAN WHO ENTERED
THE BEAUTY CONTEST
WAS EXPECTED TO DO.

Now arrange the circled letters to
form the surprise answer, as suggested by the above cartoon.

Print answer here: ◯◯◯◯ A ◯◯◯◯◯◯

JUMBLE.

Unscramble these four Jumbles,
one letter to each square, to form
four ordinary words.

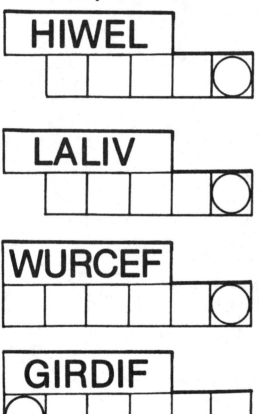

HIWEL

LALIV

WURCEF

GIRDIF

It's outdoors
weather
today

NOT MANY ARE TO BE
SEEN IN THE
CAFE WINDOW.

Now arrange the circled letters to
form the surprise answer, as suggested by the above cartoon.

Print answer here: "☐ ☐☐☐"

JUMBLE®

Unscramble these four Jumbles, one letter to each square, to form four ordinary words.

HESOW

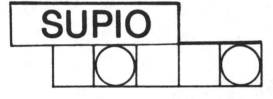

SUPIO

TREOTT

KUTBEC

WHAT CUTS IN MEDICAL CARE USUALLY CALL FOR.

Now arrange the circled letters to form the surprise answer, as suggested by the above cartoon.

Print answer here:

JUMBLE®

Unscramble these four Jumbles,
one letter to each square, to form
four ordinary words.

FINEK

VARFO

CHATED

DOHOKE

Lovely apartment

Psst, Dad,
kinda
short
this
month

THE PARENT—
ENDS UP—
PAYING IT.

Now arrange the circled letters to
form the surprise answer, as suggested by the above cartoon.

Print answer here: "  "

JUMBLE®

Unscramble these four Jumbles, one letter to each square, to form four ordinary words.

KIHCT

QUSAW

BEIMIB

WHARRO

COULD BE A QUESTION OF PRICE.

Now arrange the circled letters to form the surprise answer, as suggested by the above cartoon.

Print answer here:  ?

JUMBLE®

Unscramble these four Jumbles, one letter to each square, to form four ordinary words.

ENVIL

RASCY

SEAWEL

ABBOOM

Meet Joe . . . er . . . Bill . . . or is it Bob?

I'm HERMAN!

A NAME IS — CONFUSED — WHEN ONE CAN'T REMEMBER.

Now arrange the circled letters to form the surprise answer, as suggested by the above cartoon.

Print answer here: "  "

JUMBLE®

Unscramble these four Jumbles,
one letter to each square, to form
four ordinary words.

COAME

MYJUP

LIERIX

ERKLAT

Still at it?

BEAUTY SCHOOL

WHAT THE STUDENT
BEAUTICIAN
HAD TO TAKE.

Now arrange the circled letters to
form the surprise answer, as suggested by the above cartoon.

Answer here: A ☐☐☐☐☐ – ☐☐ ☐☐☐☐☐

Unscramble these four Jumbles,
one letter to each square, to form
four ordinary words.

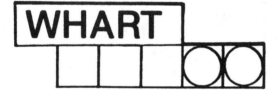
PUPER

WHART

CENNAD

LEWBIA

Guilty!

DID THE LAWYER
DO HIS BEST
IN COURT?

Now arrange the circled letters to
form the surprise answer, as suggested by the above cartoon.

Print answer here:

JUMBLE®

Unscramble these four Jumbles, one letter to each square, to form four ordinary words.

LAGED

WAMAC

ROLARP

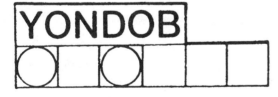

YONDOB

TRY THIS DIET IF YOU WANT TO BECOME A TIGHT-ROPE WALKER.

Now arrange the circled letters to form the surprise answer, as suggested by the above cartoon.

Print answer here: "  "

JUMBLE®

Unscramble these four Jumbles, one letter to each square, to form four ordinary words.

YONAN

GUDOH

LOICAS

RUINJY

MIGHT DESCRIBE SOME THINGS DONE IN CONGRESS.

Now arrange the circled letters to form the surprise answer, as suggested by the above cartoon.

Answer here: " ◯◯◯◯◯◯◯◯◯◯◯◯ "

JUMBLE®

Unscramble these four Jumbles,
one letter to each square, to form
four ordinary words.

HORAC

YALLD

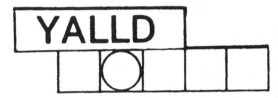

PLAICH

GREEME

REPRESENTS THE
COUNTRY — ON
PAPER, AT LEAST.

Now arrange the circled letters to
form the surprise answer, as suggested by the above cartoon.

Print answer here:

JUMBLE®

Unscramble these four Jumbles, one letter to each square, to form four ordinary words.

PHACT

DRUIL

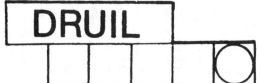
KEENAW

RETINE

How much longer?

WHAT A MODEL MAY BE WHEN UNDER A STRAIN.

Now arrange the circled letters to form the surprise answer, as suggested by the above cartoon.

Print answer here: " ⚪⚪⚪⚪⚪ "

51

MERAID
DIREAM

JUMBLE®

Unscramble these four Jumbles,
one letter to each square, to form
four ordinary words.

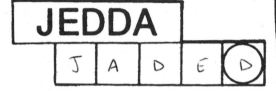

JEDDA

J A D E D

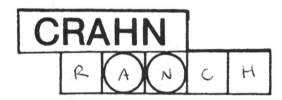

CRAHN

R A N C H

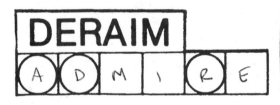

DERAIM

A D M I R E

PIDUST

S T U P I D

I own them all!

That's big business!

HOW TO CONSTRUCT AN "INDUSTRY" OUT OF NUDITY.

Now arrange the circled letters to
form the surprise answer, as suggested by the above cartoon.

Print answer here: A D D S A N D R

ANMORSD
AOOA

JUMBLE®

Unscramble these four Jumbles, one letter to each square, to form four ordinary words.

LIWLT

YUTIN

FAHBLE

GULJEG

Nothing to worry about

WHAT THEY MADE WHEN THERE WAS A POWER FAILURE.

Now arrange the circled letters to form the surprise answer, as suggested by the above cartoon.

Print answer here: ⬭⬭⬭⬭⬭ OF ⬭⬭

JUMBLE.

Unscramble these four Jumbles,
one letter to each square, to form
four ordinary words.

POZAT

KANLY

DANAGE

MOFTEN

Well ...maybe ... if ...???

ADD SOMETHING TO A "NO," AND IT MIGHT BE YES.

Now arrange the circled letters to
form the surprise answer, as suggested by the above cartoon.

Print answer here:  ☐ "☐☐-☐"

JUMBLE.

Unscramble these four Jumbles, one letter to each square, to form four ordinary words.

YANER

BICCU

GROUTH

TURUNE

Must be foreign

SEEMS TO BE A "TRICK" TO FASTENING IT.

Now arrange the circled letters to form the surprise answer, as suggested by the above cartoon.

Print answer here: A ""

JUMBLE®

Unscramble these four Jumbles,
one letter to each square, to form
four ordinary words.

LOHLE

KERCE

NERUNG

RUSSED

G'wan!

POURED ON THE
POLITICIAN.

Now arrange the circled letters to
form the surprise answer, as suggested by the above cartoon.

Print answer here:

JUMBLE

Unscramble these four Jumbles,
one letter to each square, to form
four ordinary words.

ZIMEA

INBAR

DULSHO

PLESIV

Next!

WHAT THE PRETTY
TATTOO ARTIST MADE
ON HER CUSTOMERS.

Now arrange the circled letters to
form the surprise answer, as suggested by the above cartoon.

Answer here: AN ☐☐☐☐☐☐☐☐☐☐☐☐☐

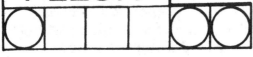

JUMBLE.

Unscramble these four Jumbles,
one letter to each square, to form
four ordinary words.

GERME

M E R G E

KICCH

C H I C K

NEPTLY

P L E N T Y

CEERUD

R E D U C E

WHAT YOU MIGHT
LIKE THE BUTCHER
TO SLICE.

Now arrange the circled letters to
form the surprise answer, as suggested by the above cartoon.

Print answer here: T H E   P R I C E

JUMBLE®

Unscramble these four Jumbles,
one letter to each square, to form
four ordinary words.

KILSY

LANVA

ENMOAB

MINTIG

AM I ABLE? COULD
BE FRIENDLY!

Now arrange the circled letters to
form the surprise answer, as suggested by the above cartoon.

Print answer here: "  "

JUMBLE®

Unscramble these four Jumbles,
one letter to each square, to form
four ordinary words.

CHALT

YIXTS

PASHIM

BLIGET

Look! He can
hardly walk!

HOW THE COPS
SPOTTED THE FENCE.

Now arrange the circled letters to
form the surprise answer, as suggested by the above cartoon.

Answer here: □□ □□□ "□□□□"

JUMBLE.

Unscramble these four Jumbles,
one letter to each square, to form
four ordinary words.

KWONN

SELLI

ODUXTE

JENTIC

WHAT HE BLAMED
HIS BAD LUCK ON.

Now arrange the circled letters to
form the surprise answer, as suggested by the above cartoon.

Answer: A ☐☐☐☐☐ AT THE ☐☐☐☐☐☐

JUMBLE®

Unscramble these four Jumbles, one letter to each square, to form four ordinary words.

PINYP

DUMON

ENGALC

REEMIP

Here, dear — you'll need a few bucks

M.D.

WHAT YOU'D EXPECT TO PAY FOR AN ACUPUNCTURE TREATMENT.

Now arrange the circled letters to form the surprise answer, as suggested by the above cartoon.

Print answer here: ⬡⬡⬡ ⬡⬡⬡⬡⬡

JUMBLE.

Unscramble these four Jumbles,
one letter to each square, to form
four ordinary words.

CASHO

VINGE

FITHES

EXNOST

Sit still!

HOW AN ANGRY
DENTIST
GRINDS TEETH.

Now arrange the circled letters to
form the surprise answer, as suggested by the above cartoon.

Print answer here:

JUMBLE®

Unscramble these four Jumbles, one letter to each square, to form four ordinary words.

KEHRI

WHOSY

PELSOG

GOHBUT

"HISTORICAL" IS THE WORD FOR THIS PRESIDENTIAL ADDRESS!

Now arrange the circled letters to form the surprise answer, as suggested by the above cartoon.

Answer here: THE ☐☐☐☐☐ ☐☐☐☐☐☐

JUMBLE.

Unscramble these four Jumbles, one letter to each square, to form four ordinary words.

WOALG

NUKKS

UPBRAL

AFDACE

Some expensive household!

ONLY ROYALTY HAVE SUCH OVERHEAD PROBLEMS.

Now arrange the circled letters to form the surprise answer, as suggested by the above cartoon.

Print answer here:

JUMBLE.

Unscramble these four Jumbles, one letter to each square, to form four ordinary words.

OPSOW

GALEL

YODMEB

BAAMEO

WHAT HE DID AROUND THE HOUSE WHEN TOLD HE WAS TOO YOUNG TO HAVE A MOPED.

Now arrange the circled letters to form the surprise answer, as suggested by the above cartoon.

Print answer here: "  "

JUMBLE®

Unscramble these four Jumbles,
one letter to each square, to form
four ordinary words.

SNAIE

EWTTE

LARNAC

NAVIED

WE DEMAND OUR RIGHTS!

NOT ODD TO BE
IN THE SEVENTIES!

Now arrange the circled letters to
form the surprise answer, as suggested by the above cartoon.

Print answer here: " ◯◯◯◯ "

JUMBLE.

Unscramble these four Jumbles,
one letter to each square, to form
four ordinary words.

PUJEL

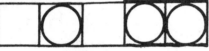
NADAP

HAPNOR

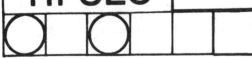
TIPSEC

WHAT BARGAIN—
PRICED CAMERAS
MIGHT BE.

Now arrange the circled letters to
form the surprise answer, as suggested by the above cartoon.

Print answer here: "  "

JUMBLE®

Unscramble these four Jumbles,
one letter to each square, to form
four ordinary words.

ECHLE

DEKIN

ENCOBA

TUSALE

An old tradition

NOT THE FIRST MAN
TO BE INVOLVED
IN A DUEL!

Now arrange the circled letters to
form the surprise answer, as suggested by the above cartoon.

Print answer here: THE ⬡⬡⬡⬡⬡⬡

JUMBLE®

Unscramble these four Jumbles,
one letter to each square, to form
four ordinary words.

HIWSS

ENPOY

NENKLE

MODEOD

URANIUM MINES

THE CROOK GOT
CHUMMY, THEN PULLED
A CONFIDENCE TRICK.

Now arrange the circled letters to
form the surprise answer, as suggested by the above cartoon.

Answer here: "◯◯◯◯-◯◯◯◯◯◯"

JUMBLE®

Unscramble these four Jumbles,
one letter to each square, to form
four ordinary words.

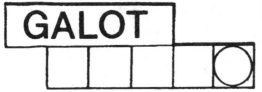
GALOT

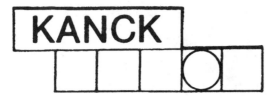
KANCK

DIPALL

NAILET

Follow me

WHERE YOU MIGHT
SLEEP WHEN YOU'RE
PUT UP FOR
THE NIGHT.

Now arrange the circled letters to
form the surprise answer, as suggested by the above cartoon.

Print answer here: THE ⬡⬡⬡⬡⬡

JUMBLE®

Unscramble these four Jumbles,
one letter to each square, to form
four ordinary words.

YIZZD

DEEXU

FIGNAC

ENBODY

MORE THAN AN
IGLOO – EVEN IF ICE
IS LARGELY USED IN
ITS CONSTRUCTION.

Now arrange the circled letters to
form the surprise answer, as suggested by the above cartoon.

Print answer here: " ☐☐ – ☐☐ – ☐☐☐ "

JUMBLE.

Unscramble these four Jumbles,
one letter to each square, to form
four ordinary words.

SOUMY

KOBOR

TRIEHD

GALEGH

WHAT THE
DERMATOLOGIST'S
BEHAVIOR WAS, TO
SAY THE LEAST.

Now arrange the circled letters to
form the surprise answer, as suggested by the above cartoon.

Print answer here: "◯◯◯◯◯"

JUMBLE.

Unscramble these four Jumbles,
one letter to each square, to form
four ordinary words.

TEGOB
◯ ◯

KECAD
◯

MIKOON
◯ ◯

NAHDEL
◯ ◯

FROM SERGEANT
TO CORPORAL!

Now arrange the circled letters to
form the surprise answer, as suggested by the above cartoon.

Print answer here: ◯◯◯◯◯◯◯

JUMBLE.

Unscramble these four Jumbles,
one letter to each square, to form
four ordinary words.

GEFUD

VANKE

LATHEC

FLUNGE

Ten years younger!

WHAT A GOOD MAKE-
UP JOB IS WORTH.

Now arrange the circled letters to
form the surprise answer, as suggested by the above cartoon.

Print answer here: ITS ☐☐☐☐☐ ☐☐☐☐☐☐

JUMBLE®

Unscramble these four Jumbles,
one letter to each square, to form
four ordinary words.

REVNY

N E R V Y

JEGUD

J U D G E

GUYSAR

S U G A R Y

WHEN SOLDIERS
DO IT THEY
USUALLY LOOK RIGHT.

FACSIO

F I A S C O

Now arrange the circled letters to
form the surprise answer, as suggested by the above cartoon.

Print answer here: " D R E S S "

EDSRS

JUMBLE.

Unscramble these four Jumbles, one letter to each square, to form four ordinary words.

JOGIN

BLEEL

STYLUB

RAKNEC

THE PART OF A WOOLEN SOCK YOU CAN SOMETIMES SEE THROUGH.

Now arrange the circled letters to form the surprise answer, as suggested by the above cartoon.

Print answer here: " ☐☐☐☐ "

JUMBLE®

Unscramble these four Jumbles,
one letter to each square, to form
four ordinary words.

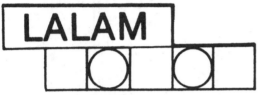

LALAM

YAASS

NATFUL

CHELEK

GA GA

WHAT LITTLE BABIES
SOMETIMES
INDULGE IN.

Now arrange the circled letters to
form the surprise answer, as suggested by the above cartoon.

Print answer here:

Unscramble these four Jumbles, one letter to each square, to form four ordinary words.

TOINX

LEETA

RAFTLE

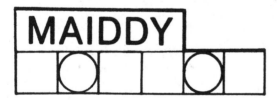

MAIDDY

IF AN ALTERATION IS REQUIRED, YOU SHOULD GET IT FROM THIS.

Now arrange the circled letters to form the surprise answer, as suggested by the above cartoon.

Answer here: A " ⬡⬡⬡⬡⬡ ⬡⬡⬡⬡⬡⬡⬡ "

JUMBLE®

Unscramble these four Jumbles,
one letter to each square, to form
four ordinary words.

HAWSS

FONTE

REFOLG

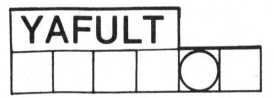

YAFULT

It's all yours!

GENERALLY LEFT
AT THE SINK.

Now arrange the circled letters to
form the surprise answer, as suggested by the above cartoon.

Print answer here: THE ⬡⬡⬡ ⬡⬡⬡⬡⬡

JUMBLE.

Unscramble these four Jumbles,
one letter to each square, to form
four ordinary words.

RAMER

TABBO

BLUJEM

CAVIDE

You're late for the game!

Washout by
the river

CRASH!

A BRIDGE
FOUNDATION THAT
MAY COLLAPSE.

Now arrange the circled letters to
form the surprise answer, as suggested by the above cartoon.

Answer here: A ⬡⬡⬡⬡ ⬡⬡⬡⬡⬡

JUMBLE®

Unscramble these four Jumbles,
one letter to each square, to form
four ordinary words.

NAWGO

SPEHE

WYLLOH

TRUSEY

Still wet behind the ears

SUCH RECRUITS HAVE
NO BUSINESS
GETTING FRESH.

Now arrange the circled letters to
form the surprise answer, as suggested by the above cartoon.

Print answer here: " ☐☐☐ " ☐☐☐☐

JUMBLE®

Unscramble these four Jumbles,
one letter to each square, to form
four ordinary words.

WHASA

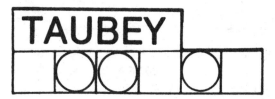
LULET

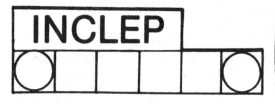
INCLEP

TAUBEY

After that
(careful!)
you'll (watch
it!) go and . . .

WHERE HIS WIFE
SENT HIM.

Now arrange the circled letters to
form the surprise answer, as suggested by the above cartoon.

Answer here: "   "

JUMBLE®

Unscramble these four Jumbles,
one letter to each square, to form
four ordinary words.

RAOAM

CHENE

SOUNIC

BROJEB

SHE WANTED THE PIN,
BUT HESITATED
TO DO THIS.

Now arrange the circled letters to
form the surprise answer, as suggested by the above cartoon.

Print answer here: "⬡⬡⬡⬡⬡⬡⬡" IT

JUMBLE.

Unscramble these four Jumbles, one letter to each square, to form four ordinary words.

ARATO

PEBID

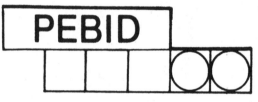

TINBAD

NAMORT

SUPERM

IT MAY BE THE CAUSE OF A KID'S RUNNING AWAY FROM HOME.

Now arrange the circled letters to form the surprise answer, as suggested by the above cartoon.

Print answer here: AN ⬡⬡⬡⬡⬡⬡⬡

JUMBLE®

Unscramble these four Jumbles,
one letter to each square, to form
four ordinary words.

YOFAR

NIXEV

SIBOPH

PHILSO

YES—IT **COULD**
"DISPEL" PAIN, SIR!

Now arrange the circled letters to
form the surprise answer, as suggested by the above cartoon.

Print answer here: "  "

JUMBLE®

Unscramble these four Jumbles,
one letter to each square, to form
four ordinary words.

REBLY

HABIS

THORAU

SNUIGE

Here! It's
all yours!

THE TAX PEOPLE
TAKE WHAT
THEY HAVE!

Now arrange the circled letters to
form the surprise answer, as suggested by the above cartoon.

Print answer here: " ☐◯◯◯ – ◯◯◯☐ "

JUMBLE®

Unscramble these four Jumbles, one letter to each square, to form four ordinary words.

GEFOB

BIMOL

YOANNE
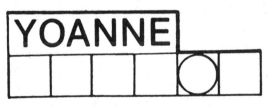

ROQUIL
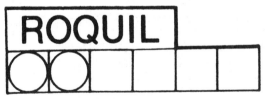

WHAT THE DENTIST'S FAVORITE DISH WAS.

Now arrange the circled letters to form the surprise answer, as suggested by the above cartoon.

Print answer here: "⬡⬡⬡⬡⬡⬡⬡"

JUMBLE.

Unscramble these four Jumbles,
one letter to each square, to form
four ordinary words.

HYSYL

TOCET

RAYPER

HEERIT

JUSTICE OF THE PEACE

WHAT USUALLY HAPPENS
WHEN PEOPLE MARRY
IN HASTE?

Now arrange the circled letters to
form the surprise answer, as suggested by the above cartoon.

Print answer here:

JUMBLE®

Unscramble these four Jumbles, one letter to each square, to form four ordinary words.

YAHND

VERBA

SPITTY

CAPELA

Oh, dear— I forgot this one

THERE'S AN EXTRA LETTER AMID "SHUFFLED" PAPERS—*MAYBE!*

Now arrange the circled letters to form the surprise answer, as suggested by the above cartoon.

Print answer here: "◯◯◯ – ◯ – ◯◯◯"

JUMBLE®

Unscramble these four Jumbles,
one letter to each square, to form
four ordinary words.

RATTI

CYRUR

INKANP

MARPHE

WHAT THE SURGEON
SAID AT THE
HOSPITAL'S ANNUAL
DANCE.

Now arrange the circled letters to
form the surprise answer, as suggested by the above cartoon.

Answer here: ⬡⬡⬡ ⬡ ⬡⬡⬡ ⬡⬡?

JUMBLE®

Unscramble these four Jumbles,
one letter to each square, to form
four ordinary words.

PIRAD

CATHY

ZIGAHN

RIQUMS

Same old
four walls
day after
day

WHAT THE BORED
HOUSEWIFE WAS
BECOMING.

Now arrange the circled letters to
form the surprise answer, as suggested by the above cartoon.

Answer here: " ☐☐☐☐ " ☐☐☐☐☐☐

JUMBLE®

Unscramble these four Jumbles, one letter to each square, to form four ordinary words.

KNUSK

BAEBY

CHURCO

DAWMOE

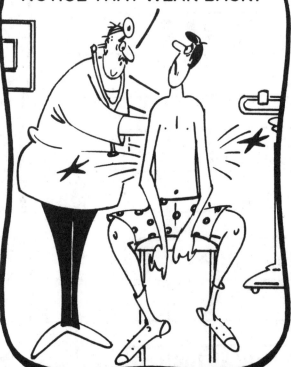

WHEN DID YOU FIRST NOTICE THAT WEAK BACK?

Now arrange the circled letters to form the surprise answer, as suggested by the above cartoon.

Answer here: "A ⬡⬡⬡⬡⬡ ⬡⬡⬡⬡"

JUMBLE®

Unscramble these four Jumbles,
one letter to each square, to form
four ordinary words.

GRITE

STOIF

AHVEBE

ELDAHN

Where are the
rest of you?

LESS THAN TWENTY
KIDS ARE IN THIS.

Now arrange the circled letters to
form the surprise answer, as suggested by the above cartoon.

Answer here:

JUMBLE®

Unscramble these four Jumbles,
one letter to each square, to form
four ordinary words.

Nope . . .we'll try
something else

THOSE MEDICINES
INJECTED BY THE
DOCTOR DIDN'T WORK.
APPARENTLY THEY
WERE ALL THIS.

Now arrange the circled letters to
form the surprise answer, as suggested by the above cartoon.

Print answer here: "  "

96

ROGIR
GRIOR

JUMBLE®

Unscramble these four Jumbles,
one letter to each square, to form
four ordinary words.

DAMAR

D R A M A

GIRRO

R I G O R

CLIPES

S P L I C E

RAWTIE

W A I T E R

WHAT THEY CALLED
THE TWINS WHO WERE
BOTH ARTISTS.

Now arrange the circled letters to
form the surprise answer, as suggested by the above cartoon.

Answer: A P A I R OF D R A W E R S

D R A W

A A R S P E I R

JUMBLE®

Unscramble these four Jumbles,
one letter to each square, to form
four ordinary words.

COEMA

GIHLT

REDDEG

PACRIY

"CLAIMED" TO MAKE SOME SORT OF POINT.

Now arrange the circled letters to
form the surprise answer, as suggested by the above cartoon.

Print answer here: "  "

JUMBLE.

Unscramble these four Jumbles,
one letter to each square, to form
four ordinary words.

ROMIN

DYNBA

KOFERD

SMIBUT

You'll never make it

ONE DOESN'T MAKE
A NAME FOR HIM-
SELF WRITING SOME-
THING THAT'S THIS.

Now arrange the circled letters to
form the surprise answer, as suggested by the above cartoon.

Print answer here:

JUMBLE®

Unscramble these four Jumbles, one letter to each square, to form four ordinary words.

CAFTE

PUJMY

GRAUSY

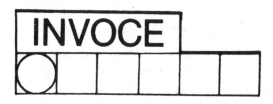

INVOCE

THESE TROUSERS SOUND BREATHTAKING.

Now arrange the circled letters to form the surprise answer, as suggested by the above cartoon.

Print answer here: "  "

JUMBLE®

Unscramble these four Jumbles,
one letter to each square, to form
four ordinary words.

TINEW

GAPAN

SCUMEL

HATTUG

He's no good for her

WHAT A GIRL
WITH A FUTURE
SHOULD AVOID.

Now arrange the circled letters to
form the surprise answer, as suggested by the above cartoon.

Answer: A ⬜⬜⬜⬜ ⬜⬜⬜⬜⬜ A ⬜⬜⬜⬜⬜

JUMBLE®

Unscramble these four Jumbles,
one letter to each square, to form
four ordinary words.

ASTEE

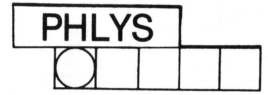

PHLYS

GATHIL

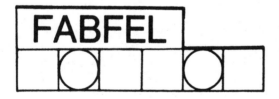

FABFEL

WHAT HE SAID
WHEN HE FINALLY
FOUND A
SHOEMAKER.

Now arrange the circled letters to
form the surprise answer, as suggested by the above cartoon.

Print answer here: "  " !

JUMBLE®

Unscramble these four Jumbles, one letter to each square, to form four ordinary words.

TUMON

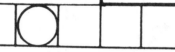

YUGEL

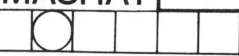

MASHAT

INQUAT

All that talk gets 'em into trouble

THINGS THAT ARE SAID ARE PUT BETWEEN THEM.

Now arrange the circled letters to form the surprise answer, as suggested by the above cartoon.

Print answer here: " _ _ _ _ _ _ _ "

JUMBLE.

Unscramble these four Jumbles, one letter to each square, to form four ordinary words.

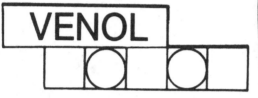

VENOL

THEFC

BLOUFE

ENGRYT

BETTER DO THIS BEFORE SPENDING LOTS OF MONEY ON A MIRROR.

Now arrange the circled letters to form the surprise answer, as suggested by the above cartoon.

Answer here:  IT

JUMBLE®

Unscramble these four Jumbles,
one letter to each square, to form
four ordinary words.

PERIT

TOSOP

ROHORR

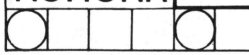

SEECIX

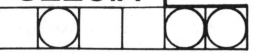

A WELL-KNOWN
WESTERN
SETTLER.

Now arrange the circled letters to
form the surprise answer, as suggested by the above cartoon.

Answer: THE ☐☐☐ – ☐☐☐☐☐☐☐☐

JUMBLE.

Unscramble these four Jumbles,
one letter to each square, to form
four ordinary words.

KLANB

ARRIF

PEEXOS

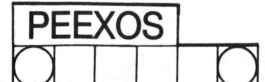

GANDOR

WHAT THE FIRST
ONE IN THE
BATHTUB WAS.

Now arrange the circled letters to
form the surprise answer, as suggested by the above cartoon.

Answer: THE " ⬭⬭⬭⬭⬭ " ⬭⬭⬭⬭⬭⬭⬭

JUMBLE.

Unscramble these four Jumbles,
one letter to each square, to form
four ordinary words.

PUTER

FENTO

MESECH

NOMOIK

WHAT THAT SHORT
DANCING TEACHER
HAD TO DO.

Now arrange the circled letters to
form the surprise answer, as suggested by the above cartoon.

Answer: ⭘⭘⭘⭘ ⭘⭘ HIS ⭘⭘⭘⭘

JUMBLE®

Unscramble these four Jumbles,
one letter to each square, to form
four ordinary words.

THIRM
○ ○ ○○ ○

MILIT
○ ○ ○ ○

BLABED
○ ○

ENKASH
○ ○ ○ ○

WHAT BUYING
A SUIT FOR
HIM WAS.

Now arrange the circled letters to
form the surprise answer, as suggested by the above cartoon.

Answer: NO ○○○○○ ○○○○○○

JUMBLE®

Unscramble these four Jumbles,
one letter to each square, to form
four ordinary words.

INBOR

RINDE

GYFFIE

GRIDIF

HOW THE
AUCTIONEER
LOOKED.

Now arrange the circled letters to
form the surprise answer, as suggested by the above cartoon.

Answer: "☐☐☐ - ☐☐☐☐☐☐☐☐☐"

JUMBLE.

Unscramble these four Jumbles, one letter to each square, to form four ordinary words.

TRAYP

WESHO

SATTEE

VERDIF

WHAT YOU MIGHT GET FROM A WAITRESS.

Now arrange the circled letters to form the surprise answer, as suggested by the above cartoon.

Answer here: "◯ ◯◯◯◯, ◯◯◯"

JUMBLE®

Unscramble these four Jumbles,
one letter to each square, to form
four ordinary words.

YARPH

HAFFC

GISTED

GLENET

WHAT THE BALLET
DANCERS SHOULDN'T
HAVE NAMED
THEIR DAUGHTER.

Now arrange the circled letters to
form the surprise answer, as suggested by the above cartoon.

Print answer here:

JUMBLE.

Unscramble these four Jumbles,
one letter to each square, to form
four ordinary words.

TIFED

CHARN

DRAPEA

BEMMER

WHAT A NEAT
MAID MIGHT BE.

Now arrange the circled letters to
form the surprise answer, as suggested by the above cartoon.

Print answer here: "  "

JUMBLE®

Unscramble these four Jumbles,
one letter to each square, to form
four ordinary words.

YEDIT

SUROE

POOSUR

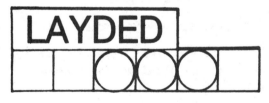

LAYDED

It's
shaky!

THEY OPEN TO
LET PEOPLE
GO UP.

Now arrange the circled letters to
form the surprise answer, as suggested by the above cartoon.

Answer:

JUMBLE.

Unscramble these four Jumbles, one letter to each square, to form four ordinary words.

DUGIE

LECEX

BOIDUT

CROGED

I need the rest

ASKED FOR BREAKFAST IN BED.

Now arrange the circled letters to form the surprise answer, as suggested by the above cartoon.

Print answer here: 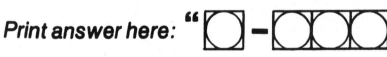 " ◯ – ◯◯◯ – ◯◯ "

JUMBLE.

Unscramble these four Jumbles, one letter to each square, to form four ordinary words.

NAHEY

LARRU

HUBERC

YOGAVE

WHEN A REPAIRMAN ONLY GIVES YOU A ROUGH ESTIMATE, THE FINAL BILL MIGHT BE THIS.

Now arrange the circled letters to form the surprise answer, as suggested by the above cartoon.

Answer here:  !

JUMBLE®

Unscramble these four Jumbles, one letter to each square, to form four ordinary words.

SYTTA

TRINP

HERFIE

UNCOPE

WHAT SHE COULDN'T STOMACH.

Now arrange the circled letters to form the surprise answer, as suggested by the above cartoon.

Answer:

JUMBLE®

Unscramble these four Jumbles, one letter to each square, to form four ordinary words.

RIHAC

TREHB

EDUCAD

LOMUVE

That's the way it's going to be!!

A DECISION FROM A CLEVER DICTATOR.

Now arrange the circled letters to form the surprise answer, as suggested by the above cartoon.

Print answer here: " ◯◯◯◯◯◯◯ "

JUMBLE®

Unscramble these four Jumbles,
one letter to each square, to form
four ordinary words.

HAFIT

MAUCS

CILOPY

UNEAVE

IS THIS ANOTHER
NAME FOR THAT
CRIMINAL?

Now arrange the circled letters to
form the surprise answer, as suggested by the above cartoon.

Print answer here: "◯◯◯◯◯"

KOKPA
PAKKO
UKKAP
KAPOK

JUMBLE®

Unscramble these four Jumbles,
one letter to each square, to form
four ordinary words.

LOARS
Ⓢ O L A R

POKKA
K A P Ⓞ Ⓚ

DENEEL
Ⓝ E E D L E

HOW THE SPEND-
THRIFT CAVEMAN
ENDED UP.

WADROC
Ⓒ Ⓞ W A Ⓡ D

Now arrange the circled letters to
form the surprise answer, as suggested by the above cartoon.

Print answer here: Ⓞ Ⓝ THE Ⓡ Ⓞ Ⓒ Ⓚ Ⓢ

~~S N E O R~~

PAK
KO
OK

JUMBLE®

Unscramble these four Jumbles,
one letter to each square, to form
four ordinary words.

MEZIA

SONOW

SLUTES

CHIPUC

**HOW MUCH DOES
THAT FAT FOOL
WEIGH?**

Now arrange the circled letters to
form the surprise answer, as suggested by the above cartoon.

Answer: A "  "

JUMBLE®

Unscramble these four Jumbles,
one letter to each square, to form
four ordinary words.

UMBOX

DUGAY

NIWWON

BORREB

Gets
no
tip

WHAT A
CLUMSY MASSEUR
MIGHT DO.

Now arrange the circled letters to
form the surprise answer, as suggested by the above cartoon.

Answer: ⬡⬡⬡ THE ⬡⬡⬡⬡⬡ ⬡⬡⬡

JUMBLE.

Unscramble these four Jumbles, one letter to each square, to form four ordinary words.

NARFC

EGGRO

SUTTOM

BLUHME

WHAT A WIFE MIGHT HAVE TO DO WHEN HER IRRITABLE HUSBAND IS SICK IN BED.

Now arrange the circled letters to form the surprise answer, as suggested by the above cartoon.

Answer: [⃝⃝⃝⃝] A [⃝⃝⃝⃝⃝⃝]

JUMBLE.

Unscramble these four Jumbles,
one letter to each square, to form
four ordinary words.

CORUS

FYNAC

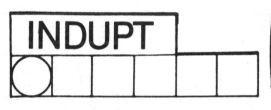

INDUPT

TASOAN

WHAT THE BUBBLE
DANCER SAID WHEN
AN ADMIRER CAME
ON TOO STRONG.

Now arrange the circled letters to
form the surprise answer, as suggested by the above cartoon.

Print answer here:

JUMBLE®

Unscramble these four Jumbles, one letter to each square, to form four ordinary words.

BUICC

LOHLE

WELLOB

MELVUL

Do you know what happens to people who sin?

THE "WRONG WAY" TO LIVE.

Now arrange the circled letters to form the surprise answer, as suggested by the above cartoon.

Print answer here: " ⬡⬡⬡⬡ "

JUMBLE®

Unscramble these four Jumbles,
one letter to each square, to form
four ordinary words.

HINEW

JARAH

NEIFED

UNPRIT

HOW THAT FIGHT
WITH THE
DENTIST ENDED.

Now arrange the circled letters to
form the surprise answer, as suggested by the above cartoon.

Print answer here:

JUMBLE.

Unscramble these four Jumbles,
one letter to each square, to form
four ordinary words.

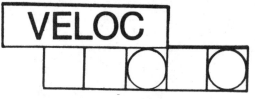

VELOC

NUDOM

NESIPP

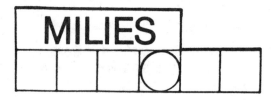

MILIES

ONE IS
"CONFUSED" BY
THIS SOUND.

Now arrange the circled letters to
form the surprise answer, as suggested by the above cartoon.

Print answer here: " ◯◯◯◯◯◯ "

JUMBLE®

Unscramble these four Jumbles, one letter to each square, to form four ordinary words.

NOYGA

TAFAL

GLYFAD

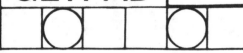

CLOWAL

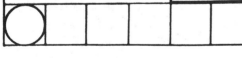

WHAT SOME PEOPLE WHO MAKE PRESERVED FRUITS AND VEGETABLES EVIDENTLY EAT.

Now arrange the circled letters to form the surprise answer, as suggested by the above cartoon.

Print answer here:  THEY "  "

JUMBLE®

Unscramble these four Jumbles,
one letter to each square, to form
four ordinary words.

TRAFC

TELLU

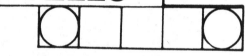

CARFIB

PHANEP

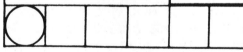

WHAT WAS THE NAME
OF THE GIRL WE
FOUND IN THE BAR?

JOE'S

Now arrange the circled letters to
form the surprise answer, as suggested by the above cartoon.

Print answer here:

JUMBLE®

Unscramble these four Jumbles, one letter to each square, to form four ordinary words.

ORGUP

ZYZUF

CORBON

TREFER

WHAT THEY CALLED THE CHIEF COOK AT THE MONASTERY.

Now arrange the circled letters to form the surprise answer, as suggested by the above cartoon.

Print answer here: THE " ⃝⃝⃝⃝⃝ "

JUMBLE.

Unscramble these four Jumbles,
one letter to each square, to form
four ordinary words.

CANEP

RUFOR

TRIUNA

INGADE

We're dealing with
a real pro

WHAT KIND OF AN
IMPRESSION DID
THE COPS HAVE
OF THE CROOK?

Now arrange the circled letters to
form the surprise answer, as suggested by the above cartoon.

Answer: A ☐☐☐☐☐☐☐☐☐☐☐☐☐☐☐

JUMBLE®

Unscramble these four Jumbles,
one letter to each square, to form
four ordinary words.

UGSIE

THOOB

SATHAG

NECKAR

SALE TODAY

Yak Yak Yak

WHAT THE TALKATIVE
BUTCHER'S "SPECIAL"
OBVIOUSLY WAS.

Now arrange the circled letters to
form the surprise answer, as suggested by the above cartoon.

Print answer here:

JUMBLE®

Unscramble these four Jumbles,
one letter to each square, to form
four ordinary words.

WROPE

NISEG

LOYMED

THACLE

HOW SHE PICKED
HER FRIENDS.

Now arrange the circled letters to
form the surprise answer, as suggested by the above cartoon.

Print answer here:

JUMBLE®

Unscramble these four Jumbles,
one letter to each square, to form
four ordinary words.

TEELI

SPAWM

BOGENY

FLAMEE

COULD BE A
LOW STORY.

Now arrange the circled letters to
form the surprise answer, as suggested by the above cartoon.

Answer here: THE ⬡⬡⬡⬡⬡⬡⬡⬡⬡

JUMBLE.

Unscramble these four Jumbles,
one letter to each square, to form
four ordinary words.

SEEPH

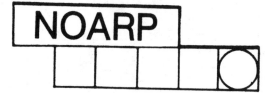
NOARP

POMLEY

PHASIM

WHAT KIND OF
A DENTIST IS
HE NOW?

Now arrange the circled letters to
form the surprise answer, as suggested by the above cartoon.

Answer here:  " ⬡⬡⬡⬡ – ⬡⬡⬡⬡ "

JUMBLE.

Unscramble these four Jumbles,
one letter to each square, to form
four ordinary words.

DUBOT

MIDUH

YILSAM

BIGNOB

WHAT SOME
PEOPLE DO TO
GET EVEN.

Now arrange the circled letters to
form the surprise answer, as suggested by the above cartoon.

Answer here:

JUMBLE®

Unscramble these four Jumbles, one letter to each square, to form four ordinary words.

VEYON

BETER

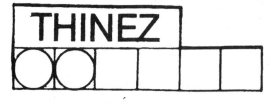

THINEZ

NISSIT

Please, Doc, DO some-thing! I'm HELPLESS!

WHERE A PROUD MAN WAS BROUGHT WHEN HE HAD HAY FEVER.

Now arrange the circled letters to form the surprise answer, as suggested by the above cartoon.

Answer here:  HIS

JUMBLE®

Unscramble these four Jumbles, one letter to each square, to form four ordinary words.

RIMEN

CHOLT

FLENNE

TOPECK

WHAT THE COPS SAID AS THEY SURPRISED THE BURGLAR.

Now arrange the circled letters to form the surprise answer, as suggested by the above cartoon.

Answer: ⬡⬡⬡⬡⬡⬡ TO ⬡⬡⬡⬡ YOU

JUMBLE.

Unscramble these four Jumbles,
one letter to each square, to form
four ordinary words.

YUNTT

HADEA

GINOUT

OLDONE

. . .an' a cup of
coffee. . .

WHAT A
CONTRIBUTION
TO CHARITY
SOMETIMES IS.

Now arrange the circled letters to
form the surprise answer, as suggested by the above cartoon.

Answer: A " ◯◯◯◯◯◯◯◯◯◯◯◯◯ "

JUMBLE®

Unscramble these four Jumbles,
one letter to each square, to form
four ordinary words.

YOIRN

CANTE

JURINE

WHERDS

THE NOT-SO-BRIGHT
FAT GUY WENT TO
THE PAINT STORE
TO GET THIS.

Now arrange the circled letters to
form the surprise answer, as suggested by the above cartoon.

Print answer here: " ☐☐☐☐☐☐☐ "

JUMBLE.

Unscramble these four Jumbles, one letter to each square, to form four ordinary words.

CLOON

NOVEY

PANUCK

RETORR

A REAL HOTHEAD! LETS YOU KNOW ABOUT GOINGS-ON UNDERGROUND.

Now arrange the circled letters to form the surprise answer, as suggested by the above cartoon.

Print answer here: A ◯◯◯◯◯◯◯◯

JUMBLE.

Unscramble these four Jumbles,
one letter to each square, to form
four ordinary words.

EGGOU

LUGBY

VIQUER

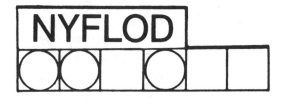

NYFLOD

He seems to be ENJOYING
his suffering

WHAT THE
HYPOCHONDRIAC'S
MOTTO WAS.

Now arrange the circled letters to
form the surprise answer, as suggested by the above cartoon.

Print answer here:

JUMBLE®

Unscramble these four Jumbles,
one letter to each square, to form
four ordinary words.

PADAT

HICCK

LEYRAR

RACCES

ARE THEY EXACT COPIES
OF THE PLACE, SIR?

Now arrange the circled letters to
form the surprise answer, as suggested by the above cartoon.

Print answer here: " ◯◯◯◯◯◯◯◯ "

JUMBLE®

Unscramble these four Jumbles,
one letter to each square, to form
four ordinary words.

SMAUE

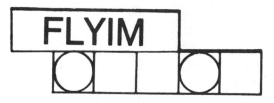

FLYIM

YALERN

TURUNE

WHAT WAS THE
DOWN PAYMENT
ON THAT
APARTMENT?

Now arrange the circled letters to
form the surprise answer, as suggested by the above cartoon.

Print answer here: A "  "

JUMBLE®

Unscramble these four Jumbles,
one letter to each square, to form
four ordinary words.

OXUMB

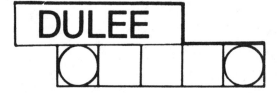

DULEE

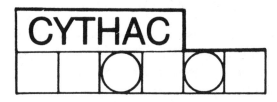

YIRRAT

CYTHAC

THIS IS A WAY-OUT
PART OF THE
MUSEUM.

Now arrange the circled letters to
form the surprise answer, as suggested by the above cartoon.

Print answer here:

JUMBLE®

Unscramble these four Jumbles,
one letter to each square, to form
four ordinary words.

SYBSA

LOVEC

DYFLAG

CHABRE

HOW HE KNEW
THE CLOCK
WAS WRONG.

Now arrange the circled letters to
form the surprise answer, as suggested by the above cartoon.

Answer: ON THE ⬡⬡⬡⬡ ⬡⬡⬡⬡ OF IT

JUMBLE®

Unscramble these four Jumbles, one letter to each square, to form four ordinary words.

YARDT

CINEW

SHUCOR

GINRAD

HOW HE WON THAT LAZINESS CONTEST.

Now arrange the circled letters to form the surprise answer, as suggested by the above cartoon.

Print answer here:

JUMBLE®

Unscramble these four Jumbles,
one letter to each square, to form
four ordinary words.

KOYSM

VABOE

FRAITY

REFLAT

Get someone in to cook
in the morning

IF YOU BREAK AN
ARM, SOMEONE MIGHT
HAVE TO MAKE
THIS FOR YOU.

Now arrange the circled letters to
form the surprise answer, as suggested by the above cartoon.

Answer: THE "⬡⬡⬡⬡⬡ ⬡⬡⬡⬡"

JUMBLE®

Unscramble these four Jumbles,
one letter to each square, to form
four ordinary words.

FEZOR

WOYNS

GAHOME

CEETIN

DELICATESSEN

CAVIAR PATÉ TRUFFLES

SAID WITH A SMILE.

Now arrange the circled letters to
form the surprise answer, as suggested by the above cartoon.

Print answer here: ⬡⬡⬡⬡⬡⬡

JUMBLE®

Unscramble these four Jumbles,
one letter to each square, to form
four ordinary words.

YOOTS

TOISH

FUPULC

TOMSED

At this rate, we'll be nabbed
before we finish the job

WHAT A CAT
BURGLAR MUST
NEVER DO.

Now arrange the circled letters to
form the surprise answer, as suggested by the above cartoon.

Answer here:

JUMBLE.

Unscramble these four Jumbles, one letter to each square, to form four ordinary words.

ROARB

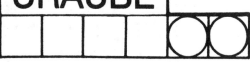

TUFOL

URAUBE

KOTLEC

IF YOU'RE SUFFERING FROM LARYNGITIS, YOU'D BEST NOT DO THIS.

Now arrange the circled letters to form the surprise answer, as suggested by the above cartoon.

Answer here:  IT

JUMBLE®

Unscramble these four Jumbles,
one letter to each square, to form
four ordinary words.

GUNTS

OGGRE

HUBLES

WAHELI

Nice day

It'll probably rain

THE PESSIMIST HUNG
AROUND THE DELI-
CATESSEN LOOKING
FOR THIS.

Now arrange the circled letters to
form the surprise answer, as suggested by the above cartoon.

Print answer here: THE " ⬡⬡⬡⬡⬡ "

JUMBLE.

Unscramble these four Jumbles,
one letter to each square, to form
four ordinary words.

PERAP

KOBOR

VERREE

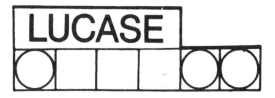

LUCASE

Hope he gets it
right this time

WHAT THEY CALLED
THE MUSIC
LIBRARIAN.

Now arrange the circled letters to
form the surprise answer, as suggested by the above cartoon.

Answer: THE ⬡⬡⬡⬡⬡⬡⬡⬡⬡⬡⬡⬡

JUMBLE.

Unscramble these four Jumbles,
one letter to each square, to form
four ordinary words.

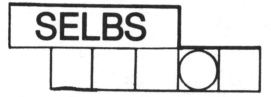

SELBS

WODDY

PHOONC

WEFURC

WHAT THE KID WHO
SAID HE DIDN'T
LIKE ALPHABET SOUP
ENDED UP EATING.

Now arrange the circled letters to
form the surprise answer, as suggested by the above cartoon.

Answer here: HIS

JUMBLE®

Unscramble these four Jumbles,
one letter to each square, to form
four ordinary words.

TYTUP

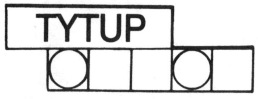

TASID

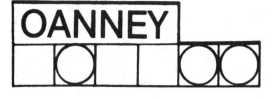

OANNEY

DRAMOR

WHAT THE INVISIBLE
MAN'S MOTHER OR
FATHER MUST
HAVE BEEN.

Now arrange the circled letters to
form the surprise answer, as suggested by the above cartoon.

Answer: A "◯◯◯◯◯ – ◯◯◯◯◯◯"

JUMBLE®

Unscramble these four Jumbles,
one letter to each square, to form
four ordinary words.

ALCKO

NEMIR

NABACA

CECHIT

THOSE FAMOUS
SCULPTURES WERE
SURE SOMETHING
TO THIS.

Now arrange the circled letters to
form the surprise answer, as suggested by the above cartoon.

Print answer here: " ◯◯◯◯◯◯◯ " ◯◯

JUMBLE.

Unscramble these four Jumbles, one letter to each square, to form four ordinary words.

WULAF

DEEGH

YELMIT

BELEEF

WHAT'S A CATTLE RUSTLER?

Now arrange the circled letters to form the surprise answer, as suggested by the above cartoon.

Answer here: A

JUMBLE®

Unscramble these four Jumbles,
one letter to each square, to form
four ordinary words.

NOUCE

YADIL

HUTORF

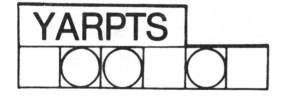

YARPTS

WHAT THEY CALLED
THAT INTELLECTUAL
HOBO.

Now arrange the circled letters to
form the surprise answer, as suggested by the above cartoon.

Answer: THE "⬡⬡⬡⬡⬡ ⬡⬡⬡⬡⬡⬡⬡⬡"

JUMBLE.

Unscramble these four Jumbles,
one letter to each square, to form
four ordinary words.

SAGYS

LUCCK

STAARY

CEIVED

A GLUTTON OFTEN
EATS MORE THAN
AT OTHER TIMES
BUT SELDOM THIS.

Now arrange the circled letters to
form the surprise answer, as suggested by the above cartoon.

Print answer here:

JUMBLE.

Unscramble these four Jumbles,
one letter to each square, to form
four ordinary words.

SNAPY

MYDUP

RUGLAF

KOJECY

That's what I get for
going on a blind date

WHAT SHE SAID
ABOUT THAT
DISAPPOINTING
LETTER CARRIER.

Now arrange the circled letters to
form the surprise answer, as suggested by the above cartoon.

Answer here: ◯◯◯◯ " ◯◯◯◯ " !

JUMBLE®

Unscramble these four Jumbles, one letter to each square, to form four ordinary words.

REZIP

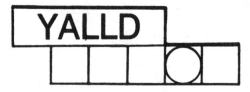

YALLD

YELLIK

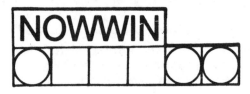

NOWWIN

To my beloved cousin Abernathy, I bequeath the sum of ten million dollars

A LEGACY IS ONE WAY OF PROVING THAT POVERTY CAN BE OVERCOME BY THIS.

Now arrange the circled letters to form the surprise answer, as suggested by the above cartoon.

Answer here:

JUMBLE.

Unscramble these four Jumbles, one letter to each square, to form four ordinary words.

ENZOO

OBOAT

MILGRY

RUMIAD

THEY WERE PARTICIPANTS IN A SHOTGUN WEDDING.

Now arrange the circled letters to form the surprise answer, as suggested by the above cartoon.

Answer: THE ☐☐☐☐☐ & "☐☐☐☐☐"

JUMBLE.

Unscramble these four Jumbles,
one letter to each square, to form
four ordinary words.

SPAWM

GEELY

UPTYDE

NOOBBA

A LOAFER IS
ALWAYS READY
TO DO THIS, TO
SAY THE LEAST.

Now arrange the circled letters to
form the surprise answer, as suggested by the above cartoon.

Print answer here: THE ⬡⬡⬡⬡⬡

JUMBLE®

Unscramble these four Jumbles, one letter to each square, to form four ordinary words.

RIVOY

RARBI

THINEW

COTESK

THE FIREMAN IS JUST ABOUT THE ONLY CIVIL SERVANT YOU'D PREFER TO SEE THIS WAY.

Now arrange the circled letters to form the surprise answer, as suggested by the above cartoon.

Print answer here:

⬡⬡⬡ AT ⬡⬡⬡⬡⬡

JUMBLE®

Unscramble these four Jumbles,
one letter to each square, to form
four ordinary words.

IPSOE

TUISE

HERNUT

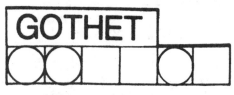

GOTHET

Curses! — Saved!

SOMETIMES THE REAL
HERO OF THE MOVIE
IS THE ONE WHO
DOES THIS.

Now arrange the circled letters to
form the surprise answer, as suggested by the above cartoon.

Answer: ⬡⬡⬡⬡ ⬡⬡⬡⬡⬡⬡⬡ IT

JUMBLE®

Unscramble these four Jumbles,
one letter to each square, to form
four ordinary words.

SELOU

RETIG

DIEPIT

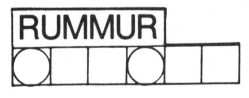

RUMMUR

WHAT THE SAD
TREE SAID AFTER
THE AXMAN DID
HIS WORK.

Now arrange the circled letters to
form the surprise answer, as suggested by the above cartoon.

Answer here:

JUMBLE

Unscramble these four Jumbles,
one letter to each square, to form
four ordinary words.

NADDY

LUFOR

INPACT

CLOTUC

WHAT THE GUY WHO
CONSTANTLY DRANK
HOT CHOCOLATE
MUST HAVE BEEN.

Now arrange the circled letters to
form the surprise answer, as suggested by the above cartoon.

Answer here: A " ⬡⬡⬡⬡⬡ ⬡⬡⬡ "

JUMBLE.

Unscramble these six Jumbles, one letter to each square, to form six ordinary words.

MARFFI

NOMMOC

UNMEBB

BRUCHE

FLOSSI

GINDHI

A very lonely man

WHAT THE MISER KEPT.

Now arrange the circled letters to form the surprise answer, as suggested by the above cartoon.

PRINT YOUR ANSWER IN THE CIRCLES BELOW

TOO ⬡⬡⬡⬡ TO ⬡⬡⬡⬡⬡⬡⬡

JUMBLE.®

Unscramble these six Jumbles,
one letter to each square, to form
six ordinary words.

STIFIM

TEEBEL

PRAMCE

TASHAG

RIPIAM

HERDIT

If I say so myself,
I'm terrific!

WHAT THAT
EGOTISTICAL
DOCTOR WAS.

Now arrange the circled letters to
form the surprise answer, as suggested by the above cartoon.

PRINT YOUR ANSWER IN THE CIRCLES BELOW

AN "◯" ◯◯◯◯◯◯◯◯◯◯◯

JUMBLE®

Unscramble these six Jumbles,
one letter to each square, to form
six ordinary words.

WHAYNO

MESECH

ROGDEC

YINCLE

BOICED

FLATES

IS THAT "SPOOK"
WHO'S RUNNING
FOR OFFICE LIKELY
TO GET ELECTED?

Now arrange the circled letters to
form the surprise answer, as suggested by the above cartoon.

PRINT YOUR ANSWER IN THE CIRCLES BELOW

NOT A ⬡⬡⬡⬡⬡⬡ OF A ⬡⬡⬡⬡⬡⬡⬡

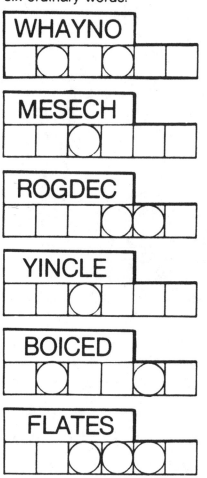

JUMBLE.

Unscramble these six Jumbles, one letter to each square, to form six ordinary words.

INTYME

HETTER

NOVCOY

DREBIG

FONLEY

LIVRIE

Here—take it all! I don't want to get into any kind of trouble with the law!

IRS

A SMART INCOME TAX PAYER KNOWS THAT IT'S BETTER TO DO THIS.

Now arrange the circled letters to form the surprise answer, as suggested by the above cartoon.

PRINT YOUR ANSWER IN THE CIRCLES BELOW

◯◯◯◯ THAN ◯◯◯◯◯◯◯

JUMBLE.

Unscramble these six Jumbles,
one letter to each square, to form
six ordinary words.

RECRON
◯ ☐ ◯ ☐ ☐

KLARET
☐ ◯ ◯ ☐ ☐ ☐

YONTUB
☐ ☐ ◯ ☐ ◯ ☐

TUMPIE
☐ ◯ ◯ ☐ ☐ ☐

UNCHAP
☐ ◯ ☐ ☐ ☐ ☐

KUPPEE
☐ ☐ ☐ ◯ ☐ ◯

AN USHERETTE
SHOULD KNOW
HOW TO DO THIS.

Now arrange the circled letters to
form the surprise answer, as suggested by the above cartoon.

PRINT YOUR ANSWER IN THE CIRCLES BELOW

◯◯◯ A ◯◯◯ IN HIS ◯◯◯◯◯

JUMBLE.

Unscramble these six Jumbles, one letter to each square, to form six ordinary words.

RAUFIN

SWOBET

YERTAW

IPCINC

GANFIC

DITNIC

PROCESSING PLANT

Shh—don't disturb him

HOW THE ORANGE JUICE PRODUCER BECAME SO SUCCESSFUL.

Now arrange the circled letters to form the surprise answer, as suggested by the above cartoon.

PRINT YOUR ANSWER IN THE CIRCLES BELOW

BY " ◯◯◯◯◯◯◯◯◯◯◯◯◯ "

JUMBLE.

Unscramble these six Jumbles,
one letter to each square, to form
six ordinary words.

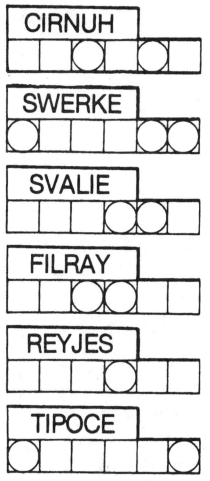

CIRNUH

SWERKE

SVALIE

FILRAY

REYJES

TIPOCE

It's a bargain at $450,000

FOR SALE

WHAT INFLATION MEANS.

Now arrange the circled letters to
form the surprise answer, as suggested by the above cartoon.

PRINT YOUR ANSWER IN THE CIRCLES BELOW

A ⬭⬭⬭⬭⬭⬭ IN ⬭⬭⬭⬭⬭⬭⬭

JUMBLE.

Unscramble these six Jumbles,
one letter to each square, to form
six ordinary words.

BABFLY

VERHIT

YAMSIL

MANCEP

OKOCIE

TANIAT

Must be in a hurry

HOW THEY ATE THAT
FANCY BANANA AND
ICE CREAM DISH.

Now arrange the circled letters to
form the surprise answer, as suggested by the above cartoon.

PRINT YOUR ANSWER IN THE CIRCLES BELOW

JUMBLE.

Unscramble these six Jumbles,
one letter to each square, to form
six ordinary words.

METROH

PARTUB

HOTSUP

FREIHE

KATINE

STOLJE

How do you manage to
stay so slim?

IF YOU WANT
TO LOSE WEIGHT,
DON'T TALK ABOUT
IT—JUST DO THIS.

Now arrange the circled letters to
form the surprise answer, as suggested by the above cartoon.

PRINT YOUR ANSWER IN THE CIRCLES BELOW

YOUR

JUMBLE®

Unscramble these six Jumbles, one letter to each square, to form six ordinary words.

MUHLIE

CUROGH

BELMAM

STANEF

ORDINO

JELGAN

WHAT A USED CAR OFTEN IS.

Now arrange the circled letters to form the surprise answer, as suggested by the above cartoon.

PRINT YOUR ANSWER IN THE CIRCLES BELOW

◯◯◯ WHAT IT ◯◯◯◯◯ TO ◯◯

JUMBLE.

Unscramble these six Jumbles,
one letter to each square, to form
six ordinary words.

RUSHOC

GUIFER

DETUIL

FORTIP

SPOMIE

DESAUB

WHAT KIND
OF A GAME IS
FOOTBALL?

Now arrange the circled letters to
form the surprise answer, as suggested by the above cartoon.

PRINT YOUR ANSWER IN THE CIRCLES BELOW

A ⬭⬭⬭⬭⬭ & ⬭⬭⬭⬭⬭⬭ ONE

JUMBLE®

Unscramble these six Jumbles,
one letter to each square, to form
six ordinary words.

WELDIM

STUJYL

EEFELC

LORCAR

WUSBAY

MULASY

WHAT GRAFFITI
ARE.

Now arrange the circled letters to
form the surprise answer, as suggested by the above cartoon.

PRINT YOUR ANSWER IN THE CIRCLES BELOW

ON

JUMBLE®

Unscramble these six Jumbles,
one letter to each square, to form
six ordinary words.

ANDAGE

BAHCLE

UNOFSI

TRINWY

TEANIN

WANEDD

WHY THEY WERE
BORED AT THE
NUDIST CAMP.

Now arrange the circled letters to
form the surprise answer, as suggested by the above cartoon.

PRINT YOUR ANSWER IN THE CIRCLES BELOW

☐☐☐☐☐☐☐ ☐☐☐☐☐ ON THERE

JUMBLE.

Unscramble these six Jumbles, one letter to each square, to form six ordinary words.

RELENK

SEKTAG

FATOLA

MIBBIE

SMUCLY

CARPHE

Sniff

WHAT A GOOD WEATHERMAN IS SUPPOSED TO BE.

Now arrange the circled letters to form the surprise answer, as suggested by the above cartoon.

PRINT YOUR ANSWER IN THE CIRCLES BELOW

A ⬡⬡⬡⬡⬡ "⬡⬡⬡⬡⬡⬡⬡"

JUMBLE.

Unscramble these six Jumbles,
one letter to each square, to form
six ordinary words.

EPALUG

LADLAB

GLACEY

DYLGOO

WEABER

VISTEN

WHY THE HEIRS WERE
NOT SURPRISED WHEN
THE WILL WAS READ.

Now arrange the circled letters to
form the surprise answer, as suggested by the above cartoon.

PRINT YOUR ANSWER IN THE CIRCLES BELOW

IT WAS A

JUMBLE®

Unscramble these six Jumbles,
one letter to each square, to form
six ordinary words.

ROOHRR

GLYFAD

TULFIE

NEEXTT

NOCHOP

SORABB

Don't you think we
should call a
professional?

HOW SOME DO-IT-
YOURSELF FREAKS
ALWAYS SEEM
TO FIX THINGS.

Now arrange the circled letters to
form the surprise answer, as suggested by the above cartoon.

PRINT YOUR ANSWER IN THE CIRCLES BELOW

Answers

1. **Jumbles**: SNARL GUMBO FROLIC BISECT
   Answer: What the neurosurgeon's idea was—
   A BRAINSTORM

2. **Jumbles**: OWING DIRTY JURIST STOOGE
   Answer: How the pretzel maker got his alibi—TWISTED

3. **Jumbles**: MURKY WHINE LACKEY PLOWED
   Answer: What the snake in the grass did when he was caught in the act—WORMED HIS WAY OUT

4. **Jumbles**: ETUDE SURLY BECALM FORAGE
   Answer: How the portrait painter expressed himself—
   HE MADE FACES

5. **Jumbles**: DECRY JUMBO INFUSE TAUGHT
   Answer: This could be the difference between male and female—AN ARGUMENT

6. **Jumbles**: CHIME HOARY SKEWER AGHAST
   Answer: Some GI's consider this the sloppiest part of the Army—THE MESS

7. **Jumbles**: MOCHA PLUME JANGLE FIASCO
   Answer: Why they called the dizzy blonde "Bubble Head"—SHE WAS ALWAYS SHAMPOOING

8. **Jumbles**: HOVEL PLAIT CREATE SOLACE
   Answer: This can be irritating as well as foolish—RASH

9. **Jumbles**: AUGUR CHIDE BUTLER LUNACY
   Answer: This might mean nothing's been taken in—
   HUNGER

10. **Jumbles**: TWILL BOOTY KNIGHT JETSAM
    Answer: What the frustrated artist drew—A BLANK

11. **Jumbles**: HITCH STAID DULCET JITNEY
    Answer: This gets longer every time you cut it—A DITCH

12. **Jumbles**: GIVEN SHOWY WEDGED BEATEN
    Answer: This often covers a lot!—WEEDS

13. **Jumbles**: CHUTE FAUNA SUBMIT TURGID
    Answer: Where a pedestrian might feel on edge—
    AT THE CURB

14. **Jumbles**: CREEL IRATE BELLOW VENDOR
    Answer: This guy might tell you a story with a slant to it—ONE WHO'S NOT ON THE LEVEL

15. **Jumbles**: LITHE PILOT STANZA GARISH
    Answer: What you might find in that ol' swimmin' hole—"STRIP-LINGS"

16. **Jumbles**: MANLY ENJOY WIDEST SOIREE
    Answer: When mother saw the bathroom she said this—"WATER MESS!"

17. **Jumbles**: VALUE DOUGH CELERY GUITAR
    Answer: What a cravat tycoon might expect plenty of from the new wide styles—GRAVY

18. **Jumbles**: JUROR MUSIC DISOWN UTMOST
    Answer: Gossip can be a pain when it's this—
    RUMOR-TISM

19. **Jumbles**: FAIRY HUMID POTENT TYCOON
    Answer: What a guy who got cold feet before the wedding did—HOTFOOTED IT

20. **Jumbles**: HANDY ACRID CHROME EYEFUL
    Answer: Language spoken by the psychiatrist's patient—"COUCHED"

21. **Jumbles**: PANIC GLEAM SURELY UNSEAT
    Answer: How the clown in the geology class defined "bedrock"—"MUSIC TO SLEEP BY"

22. **Jumbles**: GAVEL BORAX ENZYME LOTION
    Answer: The delicatessen man's wife summed up his alibi in one word—"BALONEY!"

23. **Jumbles**: ADULT INLET WALRUS PLAQUE
    Answer: How he produced oil—WELL

24. **Jumbles**: LAPEL BLESS COOPER HAPPEN
    Answer: How the banana tycoon lost a lawsuit—
    ON A PEEL

25. **Jumbles**: BOGEY HONEY AROUSE BUTTER
    Answer: What they were in the nursery—
    HUNGRY AS BARES

26. **Jumbles**: TARDY SHEEP AMAZON PURITY
    Answer: What the butcher turned actor got—
    MEATY PARTS

27. **Jumbles**: BROIL NOVEL PALACE RABBIT
    Answer: What the baby who first saw the light of day on a plane was—"AIR-BORN"

28. **Jumbles**: ARMOR BULLY DEFAME HARBOR
    Answer: The alcoholic actor's favorite sandwich—
    HAM ON RYE

29. **Jumbles**: LOOSE CAMEL FALTER EXCITE
    Answer: What a fat man in a telephone booth might suggest—A CLOSE CALL

30. **Jumbles**: ALIVE SKUNK DEMURE OPPOSE
    Answer: What a little soft soap can make—A MAN SLIP

31. **Jumbles**: CAMEO TEMPO CABANA POETIC
    Answer: What some politicians seem to want to tax most—OUR PATIENCE

32. **Jumbles**: CURIO STOKE HOTBED DETAIN
    Answer: The debtor's motto—"DUE UNTO OTHERS"

33. **Jumbles**: WOMEN BOUND WISDOM GADFLY
    Answer: Lying like this can be easy—DOWN

34. **Jumbles**: COCOA ANNOY PILFER ELICIT
    Answer: In the long run, this will benefit a writer!—
    A PLAY

35. **Jumbles**: BANJO FEVER LIKELY VANITY
    Answer: What the story of the belly dancer was—
    A NAVEL NOVEL

36. **Jumbles**: GLOAT HAIRY TURNIP SEETHE
    Answer: To get a heavy date wear this—
    SOMETHING LIGHT

37. **Jumbles**: PEACE SAVOR CORPSE MAROON
    Answer: This can make a hash of marriage—SCRAPS

38. **Jumbles**: MAKER FRANC LOTION HAMPER
    Answer: What a Crimean became after receiving his citizenship papers—"AMERICAN"

39. **Jumbles**: BRIBE WHOOP SIZZLE CAMPER
    Answer: What the policewoman who entered the beauty contest was expected to do—COP A PRIZE

40. **Jumbles**: WHILE VILLA CURFEW FRIGID
    Answer: Not many are to be seen in the cafe window—"A FEW"

41. **Jumbles**: WHOSE PIOUS TOTTER BUCKET
    Answer: What cuts in medical care usually call for—STITCHES

42. **Jumbles**: KNIFE FAVOR DETACH HOOKED
    Answer: The parent—ends up—paying it—"RENT"

43. **Jumbles**: THICK SQUAW IMBIBE HARROW
    Answer: Could be a question of price—HOW MUCH?

44. **Jumbles**: LIVEN SCARY WEASEL BAMBOO
    Answer: A name is—confused—when one can't remember—"AMNESIA"

45. **Jumbles**: CAMEO JUMPY ELIXIR TALKER
    Answer: What the student beautician had to take—
    A MAKE-UP EXAM

46. **Jumbles**: UPPER WRATH CANNED BEWAIL
    Answer: Did the lawyer do his best in court?—
    HE "TRIED"

47. **Jumbles**: GLADE MACAW PARLOR NOBODY
Answer: Try this diet if you want to become a tightrope walker—"BALANCED"

48. **Jumbles**: ANNOY DOUGH SOCIAL INJURY
Answer: Might describe some things done in Congress—"INCONGRUOUS"

49. **Jumbles**: ROACH DALLY CALIPH EMERGE
Answer: Represents the country—on paper, at least—A MAP

50. **Jumbles**: PATCH LURID WEAKEN ENTIRE
Answer: What a model may be when under a strain—"DRAWN"

51. **Jumbles**: JADED RANCH ADMIRE STUPID
Answer: How to construct an "industry" out of nudity—ADD S AND R

52. **Jumbles**: TWILL UNITY BEHALF JUGGLE
Answer: What they made when there was a power failure—LIGHT OF IT

53. **Jumbles**: TOPAZ LANKY AGENDA FOMENT
Answer: Add something to a "no," and it might be yes—A "NO-D"

54. **Jumbles**: YEARN CUBIC TROUGH UNTRUE
Answer: Seems to be a "trick" to fastening it—A "CATCH"

55. **Jumbles**: HELLO CREEK GUNNER DURESS
Answer: Poured on the politician—SCORN

56. **Jumbles**: MAIZE BRAIN SHOULD PELVIS
Answer: What the pretty tattoo artist made on her customers—AN IMPRESSION

57. **Jumbles**: MERGE CHICK PLENTY REDUCE
Answer: What you might like the butcher to slice—THE PRICE

58. **Jumbles**: SILKY NAVAL BEMOAN TIMING
Answer: "Am I able? Could be friendly!"—"AMIABLE"

59. **Jumbles**: LATCH SIXTY MISHAP GIBLET
Answer: How the cops spotted the fence—BY HIS "GAIT"

60. **Jumbles**: KNOWN LISLE TUXEDO INJECT
Answer: What he blamed his bad luck on—A JINX AT THE LINKS

61. **Jumbles**: NIPPY MOUND GLANCE EMPIRE
Answer: What you'd expect to pay for an acupuncture treatment—PIN MONEY

62. **Jumbles**: CHAOS GIVEN FETISH SEXTON
Answer: How an angry dentist grinds teeth—HE GNASHES

63. **Jumbles**: HIKER SHOWY GOSPEL BOUGHT
Answer: "Historical" is the word for this Presidential address!—THE WHITE HOUSE

64. **Jumbles**: AGLOW SKUNK BURLAP FACADE
Answer: Only royalty have such overhead problems—CROWNS

65. **Jumbles**: SWOOP LEGAL EMBODY AMOEBA
Answer: What he did around the house when told he was too young to have a moped—MOPED

66. **Jumbles**: ANISE TWEET CARNAL INVADE
Answer: Not odd to be in the seventies!—"EVEN"

67. **Jumbles**: JULEP PANDA ORPHAN SEPTIC
Answer: What bargain-priced cameras might be—"SNAPPED" UP

68. **Jumbles**: LEECH INKED BEACON SALUTE
Answer: Not the first man to be involved in a duel!—THE SECOND

69. **Jumbles**: SWISH PEONY KENNEL DOOMED
Answer: The crook got chummy, then pulled a confidence trick—"HOOD-WINKED"

70. **Jumbles**: GLOAT KNACK PALLID ENTAIL
Answer: Where you might sleep when you're put up for the night—THE ATTIC

71. **Jumbles**: DIZZY EXUDE FACING BEYOND
Answer: More than an igloo—even if ice is largely used in its construction—"ED-IF-ICE"

72. **Jumbles**: MOUSY BROOK DITHER HAGGLE
Answer: What the dermatologist's behavior was, to say the least—"RASH"

73. **Jumbles**: BEGOT CAKED KIMONO HANDLE
Answer: From sergeant to corporal!—DEMOTED

74. **Jumbles**: FUDGE KNAVE CHALET ENGULF
Answer: What a good make-up job is worth—ITS FACE VALUE

75. **Jumbles**: NERVY JUDGE SUGARY FIASCO
Answer: When soldiers do it they usually look right—"DRESS" (dress right)

76. **Jumbles**: JINGO BELLE SUBTLY CANKER
Answer: The part of a woolen sock you can sometimes see through—"LENS"

77. **Jumbles**: LLAMA ASSAY FLAUNT HECKLE
Answer: What little babies sometimes indulge in—"SMALL" TALK

78. **Jumbles**: TOXIN ELATE FALTER MIDDAY
Answer: If an alteration is required, you should get it from this—A "NEAT TAILOR"

79. **Jumbles**: SWASH OFTEN GOLFER FAULTY
Answer: Generally left at the sink—THE HOT WATER

80. **Jumbles**: REARM ABBOT JUMBLE ADVICE
Answer: A bridge foundation that may collapse—A CARD TABLE

81. **Jumbles**: WAGON SHEEP WHOLLY SURETY
Answer: Such recruits have no business getting fresh—"RAW" ONES

82. **Jumbles**: AWASH TULLE PENCIL BEAUTY
Answer: Where his wife sent him—"UP THE WALL"

83. **Jumbles**: AROMA HENCE COUSIN JOBBER
Answer: She wanted the pin, but hesitated to do this—"BROOCH" IT

84. **Jumbles**: AORTA BIPED BANDIT MATRON
Answer: It may be the cause of a kid's running away from home—AN ERRAND

85. **Jumbles**: FORAY VIXEN BISHOP POLISH
Answer: "Yes—it COULD "dispel" pain, sir!"—"ASPIRIN"

86. **Jumbles**: BERYL SAHIB AUTHOR GENIUS
Answer: The tax people take what they have!—"THE-IRS"

87. **Jumbles**: BEFOG LIMBO ANYONE LIQUOR
Answer: What the dentist's favorite dish was—"FILLING"

88. **Jumbles**: SHYLY OCTET PRAYER EITHER
Answer: What usually happens when people marry in haste?—THEY ELOPE

89. **Jumbles**: HANDY BRAVE TYPIST PALACE
Answer: There's an extra letter amid "shuffled" papers—MAYBE!—"PER-H-APS"

90. **Jumbles**: TRAIT CURRY NAPKIN HAMPER
Answer: What the surgeon said at the hospital's annual dance—MAY I CUT IN?

91. **Jumbles**: RAPID YACHT HAZING SQUIRM
Answer: What the bored housewife was becoming—"STIR" CRAZY

92. **Jumbles**: SKUNK ABBEY CROUCH MEADOW
Answer: "When did you first notice that weak back?"—"A WEEK BACK"

93. **Jumbles**: TIGER FOIST BEHAVE HANDLE
Answer: Less than twenty kids are in this—THEIR TEENS

94. **Jumbles**: IDIOT VAGUE BANTER ANKLET
Answer: Those medicines injected by the doctor didn't work. Apparently they were all this—IN "VEIN"

95. **Jumbles**: DRAMA RIGOR SPLICE WAITER
    Answer: What they called the twins who were both artists—A PAIR OF DRAWERS

96. **Jumbles**: CAMEO LIGHT DREDGE PIRACY
    Answer: "Claimed" to make some sort of point—"DECIMAL"

97. **Jumbles**: MINOR BANDY FORKED SUBMIT
    Answer: One doesn't make a name for himself writing something that's this—ANONYMOUS

98. **Jumbles**: FACET JUMPY SUGARY NOVICE
    Answer: These trousers sound breath taking—"PANTS"

99. **Jumbles**: TWINE PAGAN MUSCLE TAUGHT
    Answer: What a girl with a future should avoid—A MAN WITH A PAST

100. **Jumbles**: TEASE SYLPH ALIGHT BAFFLE
    Answer: What he said when he finally found a shoemaker—AT "LAST"!

101. **Jumbles**: MOUNT GLUEY ASTHMA QUAINT
    Answer: Things that are said are put between them—"QUOTES"

102. **Jumbles**: NOVEL FETCH BEFOUL GENTRY
    Answer: Better do this before spending lots of money on a mirror—REFLECT ON IT

103. **Jumbles**: TRIPE STOOP HORROR EXCISE
    Answer: A well-known western settler—THE SIX-SHOOTER

104. **Jumbles**: BLANK FRIAR EXPOSE DRAGON
    Answer: What the first one in the bathtub was—THE "RING" LEADER

105. **Jumbles**: ERUPT OFTEN SCHEME KIMONO
    Answer: What that short dancing teacher had to do—KEEP ON HIS TOES

106. **Jumbles**: MIRTH LIMIT DABBLE SHAKEN
    Answer: What buying a suit for him was—NO SMALL MATTER

107. **Jumbles**: ROBIN DINER EFFIGY FRIGID
    Answer: How the auctioneer looked—"FOR-BIDDING"

108. **Jumbles**: PARTY WHOSE ESTATE FERVID
    Answer: What you might get from a waitress—"A STEW, SIR"

109. **Jumbles**: HARPY CHAFF DIGEST GENTLE
    Answer: What the ballet dancers shouldn't have named their daughter—GRACE

110. **Jumbles**: FETID RANCH PARADE MEMBER
    Answer: What a neat maid might be—"ANIMATED"

111. **Jumbles**: DEITY ROUSE POROUS DEADLY
    Answer: They open to let people go up—STEPLADDERS

112. **Jumbles**: GUIDE EXCEL OUTBID CODGER
    Answer: Asked for breakfast in bed—"B-EGG-ED"

113. **Jumbles**: HYENA RURAL CHERUB VOYAGE
    Answer: When a repairman only gives you a rough estimate, the final bill might be this—VERY ROUGH!

114. **Jumbles**: TASTY PRINT HEIFER POUNCE
    Answer: What she couldn't stomach—HIS APPETITE

115. **Jumbles**: CHAIR BERTH ADDUCE VOLUME
    Answer: A decision from a clever dictator—"VERDICT"

116. **Jumbles**: FAITH SUMAC POLICY AVENUE
    Answer: Is this another name for that criminal?—"ALIAS"

117. **Jumbles**: SOLAR KAPOK NEEDLE COWARD
    Answer: How the spendthrift caveman ended up—ON THE ROCKS

118. **Jumbles**: MAIZE SWOON TUSSLE HICCUP
    Answer: How much does that fat fool weigh?—A "SIMPLE-TON"

119. **Jumbles**: BUXOM GAUDY WINNOW ROBBER
    Answer: What a clumsy masseur might do—RUB THE WRONG WAY

120. **Jumbles**: FRANC GORGE UTMOST HUMBLE
    Answer: What a wife might have to do when her irritable husband is sick in bed—NURSE A GROUCH

121. **Jumbles**: SCOUR FANCY PUNDIT SONATA
    Answer: What the bubble dancer said when an admirer came on too strong—"NO SOAP"

122. **Jumbles**: CUBIC HELLO BELLOW VELLUM
    Answer: The "wrong way" to live—"EVIL"

123. **Jumbles**: WHINE RAJAH DEFINE TURNIP
    Answer: How that fight with the dentist ended—IN A DRAW

124. **Jumbles**: CLOVE MOUND PEPSIN SIMILE
    Answer: One is "confused" by this sound—"NOISE"

125. **Jumbles**: AGONY FATAL GADFLY CALLOW
    Answer: What some people who make preserved fruits and vegetables evidently eat—ALL THEY "CAN"

126. **Jumbles**: CRAFT TULLE FABRIC HAPPEN
    Answer: "What was the name of the girl we found in the bar?"—"BERTHA"

127. **Jumbles**: GROUP FUZZY BRONCO FERRET
    Answer: What they called the chief cook at the monastery—THE "FRYER" (friar)

128. **Jumbles**: PECAN FUROR NUTRIA GAINED
    Answer: What kind of an impression did the cops have of the crook?—A FINGERPRINT

129. **Jumbles**: GUISE BOOTH AGHAST CANKER
    Answer: What the talkative butcher's "special" obviously was—TONGUE

130. **Jumbles**: POWER SINGE MELODY CHALET
    Answer: How she picked her friends—TO PIECES

131. **Jumbles**: ELITE SWAMP BYGONE FEMALE
    Answer: Could be a low story—THE BASEMENT

132. **Jumbles**: SHEEP APRON EMPLOY MISHAP
    Answer: What kind of a dentist is he now?—"PANE-LESS"

133. **Jumbles**: DOUBT HUMID MISLAY GIBBON
    Answer: What some people do to get even—ODD THINGS

134. **Jumbles**: ENVOY BERET ZENITH INSIST
    Answer: Where a proud man was brought when he had hay fever—TO HIS SNEEZE (his knees)

135. **Jumbles**: MINER CLOTH FENNEL POCKET
    Answer: What the cops said as they surprised the burglar—POLICE TO MEET YOU

136. **Jumbles**: NUTTY AHEAD OUTING NOODLE
    Answer: What a contribution to charity sometimes is—A "DOUGHNATION"

137. **Jumbles**: IRONY ENACT INJURE SHREWD
    Answer: That not-so-bright fat guy went to the paint store to get this—"THINNER"

138. **Jumbles**: COLON ENVOY UNPACK TERROR
    Answer: A real hothead! Lets you know about goings-on underground—A VOLCANO

139. **Jumbles**: GOUGE BULGY QUIVER FONDLY
    Answer: What the hypochondriac's motto was—GOOD GRIEF

140. **Jumbles**: ADAPT CHICK RARELY SCARCE
    Answer: "Are they exact copies of the place, sir?"—"REPLICAS"

141. **Jumbles**: AMUSE FILMY NEARLY UNTRUE
    Answer: What was the down payment on that apartment?—A "FLAT" SUM

142. **Jumbles:** BUXOM ELUDE RARITY CATCHY
Answer: This is a way-out part of the museum—
THE EXIT

143. **Jumbles:** ABYSS CLOVE GADFLY BREACH
Answer: How he knew the clock was wrong—
ON THE VERY FACE OF IT

144. **Jumbles:** TARDY WINCE CHORUS DARING
Answer: How he won that laziness contest—
HANDS DOWN

145. **Jumbles:** SMOKY ABOVE RATIFY FALTER
Answer: If you break an arm, someone might have to
make this for you—THE "BREAK FAST"

146. **Jumbles:** FROZE SNOWY HOMAGE ENTICE
Answer: Said with a smile—CHEESE

147. **Jumbles:** SOOTY HOIST CUPFUL MODEST
Answer: What a cat burglar must never do—
PUSSYFOOT

148. **Jumbles:** ARBOR FLOUT BUREAU LOCKET
Answer: If you're suffering from laryngitis, you'd best not
do this—TALK ABOUT IT

149. **Jumbles:** STUNG GORGE BUSHEL AWHILE
Answer: The pessimist hung around the delicatessen
looking for this—THE "WURST"

150. **Jumbles:** PAPER BROOK REVERE CLAUSE
Answer: What they called the music librarian—
THE SCOREKEEPER

151. **Jumbles:** BLESS DOWDY PONCHO CURFEW
Answer: What the kid who said he didn't like alphabet
soup ended up eating—HIS OWN WORDS

152. **Jumbles:** PUTTY STAID ANYONE RAMROD
Answer: What the invisible man's mother or father must
have been—A "TRANS-PARENT"

153. **Jumbles:** CLOAK MINER CABANA HECTIC
Answer: Those famous sculptures sure were something
to this—"MARBLE" AT

154. **Jumbles:** AWFUL HEDGE TIMELY FEEBLE
Answer: What's a cattle rustler?—A BEEF THIEF

155. **Jumbles:** OUNCE DAILY FOURTH PASTRY
Answer: What they called that intellectual hobo—
THE "ROAD SCHOLAR"

156. **Jumbles:** GASSY CLUCK ASTRAY DEVICE
Answer: A glutton often eats more than at other times but
seldom this—LESS

157. **Jumbles:** PANSY DUMPY FRUGAL JOCKEY
Answer: What she said about that disappointing letter
carrier—JUNK "MALE"!

158. **Jumbles:** PRIZE DALLY LIKELY WINNOW
Answer: A legacy is one way of proving that poverty can
be overcome by this—"WILL POWER"

159. **Jumbles:** OZONE TABOO GRIMLY RADIUM
Answer: They were participants in a shotgun wedding—
THE BRIDE & "GLOOM"

160. **Jumbles:** SWAMP ELEGY DEPUTY BABOON
Answer: A loafer is always ready to do this, to say the
least—THE LEAST

161. **Jumbles:** IVORY BRIAR WHITEN SOCKET
Answer: The fireman is just about the only civil servant
you'd prefer to see this way—<u>NOT</u> AT WORK

162. **Jumbles:** POISE SUITE HUNTER GHETTO
Answer: Sometimes the real hero of the movie is the one
who does this—SITS THROUGH IT

163. **Jumbles:** LOUSE TIGER PITIED MURMUR
Answer: What the sad tree said after the axman did his
work—"I'M STUMPED"

164. **Jumbles:** DANDY FLOUR CATNIP OCCULT
Answer: What the guy who constantly drank hot
chocolate must have been—A "COCOA NUT"

165. **Jumbles:** AFFIRM COMMON BENUMB CHERUB
FOSSIL HIDING
Answer: What the miser kept—TOO MUCH TO HIMSELF

166. **Jumbles:** MISFIT BEETLE CAMPER AGHAST IMPAIR
DITHER
Answer: What that egotistical doctor was—
AN "I" SPECIALIST

167. **Jumbles:** ANYHOW SCHEME CODGER NICELY
BODICE FESTAL
Answer: Is that "spook" who's running for office likely to
get elected?—NOT A GHOST OF A CHANCE

168. **Jumbles:** ENMITY TETHER CONVOY BRIDGE FELONY
VIRILE
Answer: A smart income tax payer knows that it's better
to do this—GIVE THAN DECEIVE

169. **Jumbles:** CORNER TALKER BOUNTY IMPUTE PAUNCH
UPKEEP
Answer: An usherette should know how to do this—
PUT A MAN IN HIS PLACE

170. **Jumbles:** UNFAIR BESTOW WATERY PICNIC FACING
INDICT
Answer: How the orange juice producer became so
successful—BY "CONCENTRATING"

171. **Jumbles:** URCHIN SKEWER VALISE FAIRLY JERSEY
POETIC
Answer: What inflation means—A CRISIS IN PRICES

172. **Jumbles:** FLABBY THRIVE MISLAY ENCAMP COOKIE
ATTAIN
Answer: How they ate that fancy banana and ice cream
dish—LICKETY-SPLIT

173. **Jumbles:** MOTHER ABRUPT UPSHOT HEIFER INTAKE
JOSTLE
Answer: If you want to lose weight, don't talk about it—
just do this—KEEP YOUR MOUTH SHUT

174. **Jumbles:** HELIUM GROUCH EMBALM FASTEN
INDOOR JANGLE
Answer: What a used car often is—
NOT WHAT IT USED TO BE

175. **Jumbles:** CHORUS FIGURE DILUTE PROFIT IMPOSE
ABUSED
Answer: What kind of a game is football?—
A ROUGH & FUMBLE ONE

176. **Jumbles:** MILDEW JUSTLY FLEECE CORRAL SUBWAY
ASYLUM
Answer: What graffiti are—SCRAWLS ON WALLS

177. **Jumbles:** AGENDA BLEACH FUSION WINTRY INNATE
DAWNED
Answer: Why they were bored at the nudist camp—
NOTHING WENT ON THERE

178. **Jumbles:** KERNAL GASKET AFLOAT IMBIBE CLUMSY
PREACH
Answer: What a good weatherman is supposed to be—
A STORM "SCENTER"

179. **Jumbles:** PLAGUE BALLAD LEGACY GOODLY
BEWARE INVEST
Answer: Why the heirs were not surprised when the will
was read—IT WAS A DEAD GIVEAWAY

180. **Jumbles:** HORROR GADFLY FUTILE EXTENT PONCHO
ABSORB
Answer: How some do-it-yourself freaks always seem to
fix things—BEYOND REPAIR

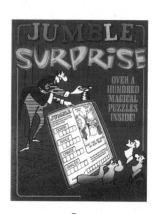